# ISLAM'S MILITANT PROPHET

# ISLAM'S MILITANT PROPHET

## MUHAMMAD AND FORCED CONVERSIONS TO ISLAM

Stephen M. Kirby Ph.D.

*Sincerely,*
*Steve Kirby*
*6.3.18*

ISBN-10: 1536892386

ISBN-13: 978-1536892383

CreateSpace
Charleston, South Carolina

# The Canon of Islam

*Islam does not, like Christianity, have a clergy. There is no temporal or even spiritual institute that holds it together or unifies it. So how has it held together—and indeed, flourished—for the last fourteen centuries approximately, when its scholars and temporal policymakers keep changing and dying out over time? How has it remained so homogeneous that the Islam of 1900 CE was doctrinally exactly the same as the Islam of 700 CE? Where have its internal checks and balances come from?*

*The answer is that Islam has a traditional canon: a collection of sacred texts which everyone has agreed are authoritative and definitive, and which 'fix' the principles of belief, practice, law, theology and doctrine throughout the ages. All that Muslim scholars (called ulema and muftis or sheikhs and imams) have left to do is to interpret these texts and work out their practical applications and details (and the principles of interpretation and elaboration are themselves 'fixed' by these texts), so that in Islam a person is only considered learned to the extent that he can demonstrate his knowledge of these texts. This does not mean that Islam is a religion of limitations for these texts are a vast ocean and their principles can be inwardly worked out almost infinitely in practice. It does mean, however, that Islam is 'fixed' and has certain limits beyond which it will not go.*

*The Muslim 500 – The World's 500 Most Influential Muslims 2016*, The Royal Islamic Strategic Studies Centre (Amman, Jordan), p. 23

# Islamic Modernism

*Islamic modernism is a reform movement started by politically-minded urbanites with scant knowledge of traditional Islam. These people had witnessed and studied Western technology and socio-political ideas, and realized that the Islamic world was being left behind technologically by the West and had become too weak to stand up to it. They blamed this weakness on what they saw as 'traditional Islam,' which they thought held them back and was not 'progressive' enough. They thus called for a complete overhaul of Islam, including—or rather in particular—Islamic law (sharia) and doctrine (aqida). Islamic modernism remains popularly an object of derision and ridicule, and is scorned by traditional Muslims and fundamentalists alike.*

*The Muslim 500 – The World's 500 Most Influential Muslims 2016*, The Royal Islamic Strategic Studies Centre (Amman, Jordan), p. 31

# Muhammad

*He* [Muhammad] *continued for more than ten years warning them by preaching, without fighting and without imposing the Jizyah and Allah commanded him to be forbearing and to patiently persevere. Then He* [Allah] *allowed him to migrate (Hijrah) to Al-Madinah and He permitted him to fight. Then He commanded him to fight those who fought against him. Then He commanded him to fight the polytheists until all and every kind of worship is for Allah (Alone).*

Muhammad ibn 'Abdul Wahhab at-Tamimi, *Abridged Biography of Prophet Muhammad*, p. 113

*Allah's Messenger remained in Makkah for thirteen years. During that time, the revelation continued being sent to him...When the evidence was established against those who defied the Messenger, Allah decreed the Hijrah. Then he ordered the believers to fight the disbelievers using swords, using them to strike the necks and foreheads of those who opposed, rejected and denied the Qur'an.*

Ibn Kathir, *Tafsir Ibn Kathir*, Vol. 9, pp. 499-500

# Table of Contents

# Introduction

*"The Koran says there is no compulsion in Islam, so no one was ever forced to become a Muslim." But on the other hand, Muhammad said...*

The idea for this book came from an exchange of e-mails that, among other things, touched on an apparent conflict between the command of Allah found in a verse of the Koran, and the actions and teachings of Muhammad, who Muslims believe spoke for Allah.

The verse in question was Chapter 2, Verse 256:

> *There is no compulsion in religion. Verily, the Right Path has become distinct from the wrong path. Whoever disbelieves in Taghut and believes in Allah, then he has grasped the most trustworthy handhold that will never break. And Allah is All-Hearer, All-Knower.*

This verse is popularly used to support the claim that there is no compulsion in Islam and no one has ever been forced to become a Muslim. There is actually much more to understanding the message of this verse than just this popular claim, and in a previous book I addressed 2:256 in more detail.[1] But for purposes of this book I am focusing on the claim that 2:256 simply means that forced conversions are not, and never have been allowed in Islam.

---

[1]     Stephen M. Kirby, *Letting Islam Be Islam: Separating Truth From Myth*, (Charleston, South Carolina: CreateSpace, 2012), "No Compulsion in Islam?" pp. 127-152.

i

However, over the centuries a number of authoritative Muslim scholars have written that on multiple occasions Muhammad himself, or through his commands to Muslim warriors, gave non-Muslims the option of either converting to Islam, being killed, or, at times, paying the *Jizyah*[2] to the Muslims. But doesn't this directly contradict the message of 2:256?

Would Muhammad really have defied Allah and made permissible what he knew Allah had made impermissible? That is not likely, because Muhammad said,

> *"Why do some people refrain from doing something which I do? By Allah, I know Allah more than they, and I am more submissive to Him than they."*[3]

Some might argue that since Muhammad would not defy Allah's commands, then these Muslim scholars were wrong. But these Muslim scholars, such as Ibn Ishaq, al-Tabari, and al-Bukhari, are among the most authoritative of Muslim scholars, and among those whose works have been relied on for centuries to better understand Islam and Muhammad. These authoritative scholars even include one who won first prize for his new biography of Muhammad in a 20th century worldwide contest sponsored by the Muslim World League, which is based in Mecca.

Muslims who know their religion understand that they condemn themselves to Hell if they lie about Muhammad. So did these authoritative Muslim scholars really lie about Muhammad and create blasphemous

---

[2]    The *Jizyah* was a tax imposed on non-Muslims living under the "protection" of an Islamic government. Such non-Muslims assumed the second-class status of *dhimmis*, with many restrictions place on them. This third option of paying the *Jizyah* was commonly applied to Christians and Jews, but over the years other groups were allowed to also pay that tax.

[3]    Muhammad bin Ismail bin Al-Mughirah al-Bukhari, *Sahih Al-Bukhari*, trans. Muhammad Muhsin Khan (Riyadh, Kingdom of Saudi Arabia: Darussalam, 1997), Vol. 9, Book 96, No. 7301, p. 246.

works of fiction?  Or, if these Muslim scholars were truthful, did the "submissive" Muhammad repeatedly defy a command of Allah?

The purpose of this book is to provide an answer to this dilemma.

The majority of the sources used in this book are English translations of authoritative works by Muslim scholars, usually translated by Muslims and published by Muslim publishing houses.

In many of the *hadiths*[4] and the Koran verses that I quote you will see words in parentheses.  These words have been inserted by the particular translator to assist the reader in better understanding the meaning of the translation.

Unless otherwise noted, the Koran verses presented in this book are from the *Interpretation of the Meanings of The Noble Qur'an*, trans. Muhammad Muhsin Khan and Muhammad Taqi-ud-Din Al-Hilali (Riyadh, Kingdom of Saudi Arabia: Darussalam, 2007).  In the footnotes I have shortened its title to *The Noble Qur'an*.

Koran verses are mentioned two ways in this book: Chapter 2, Verse 256, or 2:256.

In this book I use two different abridged English translations of the authoritative Koran commentary *Tafsir Ibn Kathir*.  Each translation was done by one or more Muslim scholars, and each was published by a Muslim publishing house.  The difference between the two translations revolves around what was abridged.  The translation published by Darussalam Publishers consists of ten volumes and covers all the chapters

---

[4]       *Hadith* (hahdeeth) (pl. *ahadith*) - A story related by a companion of Muhammad about a teaching, example, or statement of Muhammad they had personally seen or heard.  There are six authoritative collections of *hadiths*, known as the "Six Books of *Hadith*," or "The Sound Six": 1) *Sahih Al-Bukhari*; 2) *Sahih Muslim*; 3) *Sunan Ibn Majah*; 4) *Sunan An-Nasa'i*; 5) *Sunan Abu Dawud*; and 6) *Jami' At-Tirmidhi*.

of the Koran; the translation published by Al-Firdous Ltd. consists of eleven parts and only covers the Koran through Chapter 11, Verse 5.

Most of the dates used in this book are Anno Domini. There are some dates using the lunar-based Muslim calendar, and these dates are designated with "AH." The first year of the Muslim calendar began in 622, the year the small Muslim community emigrated from Mecca to Medina; this emigration was known as the *Hijrah*. Consequently, the AH stands for the Latin term *Anno Hegirae* (Year of the *Hijrah*).

Stephen M. Kirby
October 26, 2016

*As for the obligation to obey the Prophet, may Allah bless him and grant him peace, belief in him demands it. Confirmation of what he brought requires obedience to him because that is part of what he brought.*[5]

---

[5]     Qadi 'Iyad ibn Musa al-Yahsubi, *Muhammad, Messenger of Allah: Ash-Shifa of Qadi 'Iyad*, trans. Aisha Abdarrahman Bewley (Norwich, UK: Diwan Press, 2011), p. 215.

# The Dilemma

When discussing or writing about the religion of Islam it has become obligatory in many circles to conspicuously proclaim at some point that "there is no compulsion in Islam." The meaning of this is that no one has ever been forced to convert to Islam, and to force someone to do so would not be a part of Islam. And there is a verse of the Koran that is commonly used as the basis for this claim of "no compulsion":

Chapter 2, Verse 256

> *There is no compulsion in religion. Verily, the Right Path has become distinct from the wrong path. Whoever disbelieves in Taghut* [1] *and believes in Allah, then he has grasped the most trustworthy handhold that will never break. And Allah is All-Hearer, All-Knower.*

Muslims believe that the Koran consists of the timeless, perfect, and unchangeable word of Allah, so this verse of the Koran should be as valid and applicable today as it was when it was "revealed" in the 7th Century.

The Koran also states that: 1) Muhammad spoke for Allah (4:80); 2) Muslims are commanded to obey Muhammad in all things (59:7); and 3) Muhammad is the timeless standard by which Muslims should conduct themselves (33:21).

We learn about Muhammad from two main sources: 1) the numerous histories of Islam and the biographies written about him by authoritative

---

[1] *Taghut* means false gods and anything worshipped other than Allah.

Muslim scholars, starting as early as the 8<sup>th</sup> Century; and 2) the authoritative *hadith* collections.  And in many of these works we find repeated instances where Muhammad gave non-Muslims the choice of converting to Islam, being killed, or at times paying the *Jizyah*.

But how can this be when 2:256 plainly states that there is no such thing as forced conversions to Islam?

The first thought that comes to mind is that, for whatever reason, these Muslim scholars were simply lying about the statements and actions of Muhammad.  But for a Muslim, telling lies about Muhammad condemns one to the Fires of Hell.  Consider these *hadiths* from five Companions of Muhammad:

1.  *It was narrated that Abu Qatadah said: "While he was on this pulpit, I heard the Messenger of Allah saying: 'Beware of narrating too many Ahadith from me. Whoever attributes something to me, let him speak the truth faithfully.  Whoever attributes to me something that I did not say, let him take his place in Hell.'"*[2]

2.  *It was narrated that Abu Hurairah said: "The Messenger of Allah said: 'Whoever attributes to me something that I have not said, let him take his place in Hell.'"*[3]

3.  *...Ibn 'Abbas who said: "Allah's Messenger, Allah bless him and give him peace, said: 'Avoid reporting anything from me other than what you know, for whoever lies about*

---

[2]      Muhammad bin Yazeed ibn Majah al-Qazwini, *Sunan Ibn Majah*, trans. Nasiruddin al-Khattab (Riyadh, Kingdom of Saudi Arabia: Darussalam, 2007), Vol. 1, No. 35, p. 96.

[3]      Ibid., No. 34, p. 96.

*me shall be in hell fire; and whoever lies about the Qur'an shall enter hell fire.*"[4]

4. *It was narrated that 'Ali said: "The Messenger of Allah said: 'Do not tell lies about me, for telling lies about me leads to Hell (Fire).'"*[5]

5. 'Uthman Ibn 'Affan, the third Caliph, said from the pulpit:

> *Behold! I heard him* [Muhammad], *may Allah bless him, saying: He, who ascribes to me what I have not said, would make his abode in hell-fire.*[6]

The early Muslim scholars cited in this book have been considered authoritative by other Muslim scholars for centuries, and I have even included an award-winning 20th century biography of Muhammad.[7] These

---

[4]      Abu'l-Hasan 'Ali ibn Ahmad ibn Muhammad ibn 'Ali al-Wahidi, *Al-Wahidi's Asbab al-Nuzul*, trans. Mokrane Guezzou (Louisville, KY: Fons Vitae, 2008), p. 2.

[5]      *Sunan Ibn Majah*, Vol. 1, No. 31, p. 95. For similar reports by 'Ali, see Ahmad bin Muhammad bin Hanbal ash-Shaibani, *Musnad Imam Ahmad Bin Hanbal*, trans. Nasiruddin Al-Khattab, ed. Huda Al-Khattab (Riyadh, Kingdom of Saudi Arabia: Darussalam, 2012), Vol. 1, No. 629, p. 331; and No. 1127, p. 523.

[6]      Abu 'Abd Allah Muhammad ibn Sa'd ibn Mani' al-Zuhri al-Basri, *Kitab al-Tabaqat al-Kabir*, trans. S. Moinul Haq (New Delhi, India: Kitab Bhavan, 2009), Vol. 2, p. 435. For a similar report by 'Uthman, see *Musnad Imam Ahmad Bin Hanbal*, Vol. 1, No. 469, p. 265.

For additional *hadiths* about the dire consequences of telling a lie about Muhammad, intentional or not, see Abu 'Eisa Mohammad ibn 'Eisa at-Tirmidhi, *Jami' At-Tirmidhi*, trans. Abu Khaliyl (Riyadh, Kingdom of Saudi Arabia: Darussalam, 2007), Vol. 5, Nos. 2659-2660, pp. 59-60.

[7]      Safiur-Rahman al-Mubarakpuri, *The Sealed Nectar* (Riyadh, Kingdom of Saudi Arabia: Darussalam, 2008). In 1979 this biography was awarded first prize

are not reputations that would support the claim that these scholars have lied about Muhammad.

So here is our dilemma:

1.  It is commonly understood and claimed that in 2:256 the Koran states that no one should be forced to become a Muslim.

2.  The Koran also states that Muhammad spoke for Allah, must be obeyed in all things, and is considered the timeless example for all Muslims.

3.  In works written by authoritative Muslim scholars we have numerous reports of Muhammad offering non-Muslims the choice of converting to Islam, being killed, or paying the *Jizyah* (or sometimes just the choice of converting or being killed). These reports come from Muslim scholars who should know that lying about Muhammad sends a Muslim to the Fires of Hell.

4.  So are these authoritative Muslim scholars already experiencing, or soon to experience, the Fires of Hell, and should their works be considered nothing more than blasphemous fiction?

5.  Or perhaps, in spite of the verse's popularity in modern conversations and writings, the timeless, perfect words of Allah in 2:256 lost their doctrinal authority at some point and were replaced by another command?

Our first step in resolving this dilemma is to use the next two chapters to first, examine a doctrine that is fundamental to understanding the Koran, and second, to take a look at how we are to understand the messages of Koran verses.

---

by the Muslim World League in the worldwide competition for a new biography of Muhammad. The Muslim World League is headquartered in Mecca.

# The Doctrine of Abrogation (*Naskh*)

*...if two verses deal with the same topic and give different rulings, but one is madanee [Medinan] and the other is makkee [Meccan], the ruling is taken from the madanee verse.*[8]

Understanding the Doctrine of Abrogation (*Naskh*) is fundamental to understanding the Koran and Islam. The Muslim scholar al-Qurtubi wrote:

> *This subject is very important and scholars must be aware of it. Only ignorant fools deny it because of the effect of events on rulings and recognition of the halal and haram. Abu'l-Bakhtari said, "'Ali entered the mosque while a man was causing the people there to become frightened. He asked, 'What is this?' They said, 'A man who is reminding people.'...He sent for him and asked, 'Do you know the abrogating from the abrogated?' 'No,' he replied. He said, 'Then leave our mosque and do not admonish people in it.'"*[9]

In order to understand abrogation we must first get a basic understanding of the Koran. The Koran is the sacred book of Islam, and it is considered by Muslims to be the timeless, perfect, and unchangeable word of Allah;

---

[8]     Abu Ammaar Yasir Qadhi, *An Introduction to the Sciences of the Qur'aan* (Birmingham, UK: Al-Hidaayah Publishing, 1999), p. 106.

[9]     Abu 'Abdullah Muhammad ibn Ahmad al-Ansari al-Qurtubi, *Tafsir Al-Qurtubi: Classical Commentary of the Holy Qur'an*, Vol. 1, trans. Aisha Bewley (London: Dar Al Taqwa Ltd., 2003), p. 321. The *halal* is that which is permitted, and the *haram* is that which is forbidden.

Muslims believe that the Koran in Arabic is an exact copy of the book that Allah has beside him in Paradise. The verses of the Koran were delivered to Muhammad through the angel *Jibril* (Gabriel) in a series of "revelations." Muhammad started receiving these "revelations" in Mecca in 610; they continued through his emigration to Medina in 622, and ended only with his death in Medina in 632.

The Koran has 114 chapters (*suras/soorahs*). However, they are not arranged in chronological order. With the exception of the first chapter, they are arranged generally by the length of the chapter, with the shortest chapters coming at the end. For example, the first chapter, *Al-Fatihah*, has only seven verses, while the second, third, and fourth chapters have 286, 200, and 176 verses, respectively.

Translations of the Koran usually indicate whether a chapter was "revealed" in Mecca or in Medina. However, this does not automatically mean that the verse was "revealed" when Muhammad was physically in Mecca or physically in Medina. It is rather a common shorthand approach that refers to the Meccan time period (610-622) and the Medinan time period (622-632), because Muhammad received "revelations" even when he was not physically in either one of those two cities. In the Koran you will find that the chapters of the earlier "revelations" from Mecca are interspersed among chapters of the later "revelations" from Medina.

There is an important significance to when a verse or chapter was "revealed." While in Mecca, the religion of Islam was just starting and it was generally not well received. Perhaps as a result of this, the verses of the Koran "revealed" during the Meccan period were generally more peaceful and accommodating toward non-Muslims than the verses "revealed" later in the Medinan period. The verses from the Medinan period had a general tendency to be more belligerent and intolerant, and more inclined to make sharp differentiations between Muslims (believers) and non-Muslims (disbelievers/unbelievers).

This can lead to an irreconcilable contradiction between the message of a Meccan verse and that of a Medinan verse addressing the same topic. But

6

how can there be such a contradiction if the Koran is the timeless, perfect, and unchangeable word of Allah?

This was covered in a Medinan verse in the Koran that introduced the concept of "abrogation"; that is Chapter 2, Verse 106:[10]

> *Whatever a Verse (revelation) do We abrogate or cause to be forgotten, We bring a better one or similar to it. Know you not that Allah is Able to do all things?*

So if there is an irreconcilable contradiction between the messages of two "revelations" in the Koran, then the most recent "revelation" abrogates (supersedes) the earlier one and is now the one to be followed.

Consequently, a "revelation" made in the Medinan period would supersede a similar, earlier "revelation" made in the Meccan period if there was an irreconcilable conflict between the two. And if there was such a conflict between two Medinan verses, then the one "revealed" later would supersede the earlier one. Both verses remain in the Koran because they are considered the words of Allah, but it is the most recent "revelation" that now carries the doctrinal authority.

How quickly could a verse be abrogated? The answer is that it could happen in as little as one hour. Around the time period 626-627 many Muslims were coming up to Muhammad and seeking private discussions with him. It became so time-consuming for Muhammad that 58:12 of the

---

[10]    A basis for abrogation is also found in 16:101, a Late Meccan verse (for the determination of this time period, see *The Meaning of the Glorious Koran*, trans. Marmaduke Pickthall (1930; rpt. New York: Alfred A. Knopf, 1992), pp. 7 and 268):

> *And when We change a Verse (of the Qur'an) in place of another - and Allah knows best what He sends down - they (the disbelievers) say: "You (O Muhammad) are but a Muftari! (forger, liar)." Nay, but most of them know not.*

But 2:106 is the verse most commonly referred to when discussing abrogation.

7

Koran was "revealed." This verse commanded Muslims to give something extra to charity before they approached Muhammad. Even though the verse exempted those who could not afford to do so, there were still many Muslims who felt they could not afford to provide any additional charity, and consequently, many of them stopped consulting with Muhammad.

As a result, 58:13 was "revealed"; this verse allowed Muslims to replace the extra charity in 58:12 with the already established requirements of prayer, obeying Allah and the obligatory charity (*zakat*). 58:12 was in effect for only one hour before it was abrogated by 58:13; during that time 58:12 was implemented only once, by 'Ali bin Abi Talib, who gave ten "silver pieces" to charity and asked Muhammad either ten questions or one question consisting of ten words.[11]

There are four ways in which abrogation can occur:[12]

1. The Koran abrogating the Koran.

2. The Koran abrogating the *Sunnah* (the teachings and examples of Muhammad that have become rules to be followed by Muslims).

3. The *Sunnah* abrogating the Koran - The founders of three of the four major Sunni Schools of Sharia Law allowed this; they

---

[11]      Abu al-Fida' 'Imad Ad-Din Isma'il bin 'Umar bin Kathir al-Qurashi Al-Busrawi, *Tafsir Ibn Kathir* (Abridged), abr. Shaykh Safiur-Rahman al-Mubarakpuri, trans. Jalal Abualrub, et al. (Riyadh, Kingdom of Saudi Arabia: Darussalam, 2000), Vol. 9, pp. 528-531; *Tafsir Ibn 'Abbas*, trans. Mokrane Guezzou (Louisville, KY: Fons Vitae, 2008), p. 751; Salahuddin Yusuf, *Tafsir Ahsanul-Bayan*, trans. Mohammad Kamal Myshkat (Riyadh, Kingdom of Saudi Arabia: Darussalam, 2010), Vol. 5, pp. 390-391; and *Al-Wahidi's Asbab al-Nuzul*, p. 221.

[12]      *An Introduction to the Sciences of the Qur'aan*, pp. 238-240. This list of the four ways in which abrogation can occur was also noted in Ahmad Von Denffer, *'Ulum al-Qur'an: An Introduction to the Sciences of the Qur'an* (Leicestershire, UK: The Islamic Foundation, 1994), p. 82.

8

reasoned that both the Koran and the *Sunnah* were "forms of revelation from Allah" and could therefore abrogate one another.[13]

The requirement for this was that the abrogating *hadith* had to be considered *mutawaatir*; this meant the *hadith* had "been reported by many narrators and with different chains of transmission."[14] The rationale for this was that the more narrators and different chains of transmission involved, the less chance there would be for the *hadith* to be false. As the Muslim scholar al-Suyuti wrote:

> *The mutawatir is the type that is of* [sic]
> *transmitted by a group of men when there is no*
> *possibility of their conspiring to lie about their*

---

*authority, and by the likes of them to the end of transmission.*[15]

4. The *Sunnah* abrogating the *Sunnah*.

And there is another way in which the *Sunnah* can have an impact on a verse in the Koran, and vice versa: *Takhsees*.


## Specification (*Takhsees*)

Koran verses and the *Sunnah* can also be impacted by "specification" (*takhsees*), which places limitations on an earlier verse or on a particular aspect of the *Sunnah*. Yasir Qadhi explained the difference between *takhsees* and *naskh* (abrogation) in terms of Koran verses:

> *'Specification' involves one verse limiting or restricting a general ruling found in another verse, whereas naskh involves abrogating the first ruling in toto (i.e., it is not applied in any circumstances or conditions).*[16]

He noted that "after a *takhsees* occurs, the ruling is not totally invalid, but rather valid in a narrower frame."[17]

A Koran verse can be limited or restricted by the *Sunnah*. Qadhi provided an example of how *takhsees* was applied by Muhammad to the Koran verse that commanded amputation as the punishment for theft (5:38):

---

[15]  Jalal-al-Din 'Abd al-Rahman al-Suyuti, *The Perfect Guide to the Sciences of the Qur'an*, trans. Hamid Algar, et al. (Reading, UK: Garnet Publishing, 2011), p. 185.

[16]  *An Introduction to the Sciences of the Qur'aan*, p. 233.

[17]  Ibid., p. 250.

*The verse is general ('aam), and implies that the hand of
every thief must be cut. The Prophet, however, qualified
that the thief in this case must steal above a certain
monetary value. If he stole below this value, this ruling
will not apply to him. Therefore, the Prophet specified the
general ruling of the verse. This, then, is an example of
takhsees: the hand of every thief will not be cut; only those
thieves who steal above a certain monetary value are
punished.*[18]

And here we have an example in which a verse of the Koran limited the
*Sunnah.* This is an event that occurred in February 628:

*Narrated Abu Qilaba: Anas said, "Some people of 'Uki or
'Uraina tribe came to Al-Madina and its climate did not
suit them. So the Prophet ordered them to go to the herd
of (milch) camels and to drink their milk and urine (as a
medicine). So they went as directed and after they became
healthy, they killed the shepherd of the Prophet and drove
away all the camels. The news reached the Prophet early
in the morning and he sent (men) in their pursuit and they
were captured and brought at noon. He then ordered to
cut [off] their hands and feet (and it was done), and their
eyes were branded with heated pieces of iron. They were
put in Al-Harra [a place of stony ground in Medina] and
when they asked for water, no water was given them."
Abu Qilaba added, "Those people committed theft,
murder, became disbelievers after embracing Islam
(Murtadin) and fought against Allah and His
Messenger."*[19]

---

[18]     Ibid., p. 249.

[19]     Muhammad bin Ismail bin Al-Mughirah al-Bukhari, *Sahih Al-Bukhari,*
trans. Muhammad Muhsin Khan (Riyadh, Kingdom of Saudi Arabia: Darussalam,
1997), Vol. 1, Book 4, No. 233, pp. 178-179.

11

However, Allah later "rebuked" Muhammad for the extent of these punishments and a verse of the Koran was "revealed" that restricted the nature of such punishment:

> *It was narrated from Abu Az-Zinnad, that when the Messenger of Allah cut off (the hands and feet) of those who stole his camels and gouged out their eyes with fire, Allah rebuked him for that and Allah revealed (the words): The recompense of those who wage war against Allah and His Messenger and do mischief in the land is only that they shall be killed or crucified or their hands and their feet be cut off from opposite sides, or be exiled from the land. That is their disgrace in this world, and a great torment is theirs in the Hereafter.[20]*

So instead of gouging out the eyes and cutting off both of the hands and feet of an individual, punishment of that nature was now to be limited to only cutting off one hand and one foot, from opposite sides. This "revelation" from Allah was codified in 5:33 of the Koran.

Knowing that Koran verses and the *Sunnah* can be affected by abrogation and *takhsees* will help us in resolving our dilemma.

---

[20]     Abu Dawud Sulaiman bin al-Ash'ath bin Ishaq, *Sunan Abu Dawud*, trans. Yaser Qadhi (Riyadh, Kingdom of Saudi Arabia: Darussalam, 2008), Vol. 5, No. 4370, p. 26.

# Understanding Verses of the Koran

How is one supposed to understand the message of the verses in the Koran? There are some who feel that the message of each verse is subject to their individual interpretation, and that they can personally determine which verses are timeless in message and which were applicable only to the 7th Century. Such approaches can open up the possibility for as many interpretations of Koran verses as there are people in the room. But this "personal interpretation" is not the approach that has been taken over the centuries by Muslim scholars, and consequently, not the approach we will take here.

## The Principles of *Tafsir*

Our approach will involve doing what Muslim scholars and those wanting to learn about Islam have done for centuries: consulting authoritative written commentaries on the Koran (the *tafsirs*). *Tafsir* means "the explanation or interpretation of something."[21] The *tafsirs* explain the meanings and the contexts of verses in the Koran. In fact, the authoritative *tafsirs* are the primary sources for understanding the Koran.

The scholars who wrote these *tafsirs* did not use their own opinions to explain Koran verses, because this was the very thing against which Muhammad had warned:

> *Muhammad bin Jarir reported that Ibn 'Abbas said that the Prophet said, 'Whoever explains the Qur'an with his*

---

[21]     *An Introduction to the Sciences of the Qur'aan*, p. 289.

*opinion or with what he has no knowledge of, then let him assume his seat in the Fire.*[22]

They rather relied on the *Principles of Tafsir*, which are based first on consulting the Koran, then second, consulting the *Sunnah*, and then third, consulting the statements of Muhammad's Companions. The Muslim scholar al-Suyuti explained the *Principles of Tafsir* in this manner:

> *The scholars have said: Whoever wishes to interpret the Qur'aan, he should first turn to the Qur'aan itself. This is because what has been narrated succinctly in one place might be expounded upon in another place, and what is summarized in one place might be explained in another...*
>
> *If he has done that, then he turns to the Sunnah, for it is the explainer of the Qur'aan, and a clarifier to it. Imaam as-Shaafi'ee said, "All that the Prophet said is based on his understanding of the Qur'aan...*
>
> *If he does not find it (the tafseer) in the Sunnah, he turns to the statements of the Companions, for they are the most knowledgeable of it, since they witnessed the circumstances and situations the Qur'aan was revealed in...*[23]

## Two Categories of Koran Verses

Islamic Doctrine teaches that the verses of the Koran can be divided into two categories:[24]

---

[22]      *Tafsir Ibn Kathir*, Vol. 1, pp. 32-33.

[23]      *An Introduction to the Sciences of the Qur'aan*, pp. 299-300.

[24]      Ibid., p. 107.

1.  Those verses "revealed" because of a specific incident or occurrence. Such verses "must have been revealed in response to the occurrence, and give an answer or ruling pertaining to that occurrence."

2.  Those verses "revealed" without a preceding incident or occurrence. Most of the verses in the Koran were "revealed" without a particular preceding incident.

For various reasons a verse might have been "revealed" on more than one occasion, and it is possible that multiple verses were "revealed" in response to a single occasion.[25]


## Are Koran Verses Specific or General?

Now we come to a fundamental question: are the messages of Koran verses specific or general? In other words, when a Koran verse was "revealed," was its message specific only to a particular occurrence and/or time period? Or is the message of a Koran verse generally applicable without time restrictions?

There are a few Koran verses that were specific to a particular occurrence and cannot be applied generally. Examples of such verses are found in 24:11-20, which dealt with the slander of Muhammad's wife Aisha during the time period of December 627. Another example is found in 33:50, which exempted only Muhammad from the restriction of having no more than four wives (this restriction on all other Muslim men is found in 4:3). And we have 66:1-5 which dealt with Muhammad and his wives.

But with the exception of a few verses such as these, each verse is general in meaning, with no time restrictions. As Yasir Qadhi pointed out:

---

[25]     Ibid., pp. 111-116. Also see *The Perfect Guide to the Sciences of the Qur'an*, pp. 69-70, and 75-76; and *Introduction to the Principles of Tafsir*, p. 61.

*...it is not possible to restrict the ruling to the circumstances of its revelation, for the Qur'aan was revealed as a guidance for all the nations until the Day of Judgement...*[26]

This was also noted by the Muslim scholar Ibn Taymiyyah:

*Any verse which was revealed for a particular reason, especially if the verse is an order or a prohibition, not only includes that particular person for whom it was revealed but all those similar to him. This is also the case if the verse is praising or censuring someone.*[27]

And the Muslim scholar al-Suyuti wrote that the

*matter that arises in connection with verses revealed with reference to a given event or occasion is whether the general sense yielded by the wording of a verse or the specific one implied by the occasion of revelation should be given primacy...in my opinion it is the first of the alternatives that is preferable.*[28]

Now, aided by the Doctrine of Abrogation, reliance on authoritative *tafsirs*, histories, biographies, and *hadiths*, and with the understanding that most of the verses in the Koran are general in meaning and timeless in message, we will use a chronological approach to resolve what appears to be a fundamental conflict between a command of Allah in the Koran and the *Sunnah* of Allah's prophet, Muhammad.

---

[26]     *An Introduction to the Sciences of the Qur'aan*, p. 118.

[27]     *Introduction to the Principles of Tafsir*, p. 57.

[28]     *The Perfect Guide to the Sciences of the Qur'an*, p. 57.

# The Meccan Period (610-622)

The Religion of Islam began in Mecca in 610. There was a great deal of resistance to this new religion, and by the time the Muslims emigrated to Medina in 622 there were estimated to be no more than 200 followers of Muhammad.

Even with this slow growth, during this period of nascent Islam we can see the early development of three particular components:

1. Muslims were to obey Allah and Muhammad.

2. Muhammad was to be obeyed because he commanded all that was lawful and forbade all that was forbidden.

3. There was an emerging militant component to Islam: everyone would submit to Islam, whether willingly or unwillingly.

## Early Meccan Period (circa 610-615) [29]

Muhammad received his first "revelation" from Allah in 610. Shortly thereafter, his wife Khadija converted to Islam, and she was soon followed by Muhammad's young cousin Ali.

Even in these beginning days Muhammad was talking about treasures to be acquired through Muslim military conquests. Here is a report about this

---

[29]    For this chapter I am using Pickthall's categories of the Meccan time period – see *The Meaning of the Glorious Koran*, p. 7.

from an Arab merchant who briefly stayed with Muhammad's uncle, al-'Abbas:

> *I was a merchant, and I came during the pilgrimage and stayed with al-'Abbas. While we were with him, a man came out to pray and stood facing the Ka'bah. Then a woman came out and stood praying with him, followed by a youth who stood praying with him. I said, "'Abbas, what is this religion? I do not know what this religion is." He answered, "This is Muhammad b. 'Abdallah, who claims that God has sent him as His Messenger with this [religion], and that the treasures of Chusroes and Caesar will be given to him by conquest.* [30]

Chapter 53 of the Koran was "revealed" in this Early Meccan Period.[31] Three verses in that chapter set the tone for the way the Muslims were to henceforth regard Muhammad. These verses stated that Muhammad was on the right path, untouched by error, and spoke not for himself, but rather spoke only that which Allah had commanded him:[32]

Chapter 53, Verses 2-4

> *Your companion (Muhammad) has neither gone astray nor has erred. Nor does he speak of (his own) desire. It is only a Revelation revealed.*

---

[30]  Abu Ja'far Muhammad b. Jarir al-Tabari, *The History of al-Tabari: Muhammad at Mecca*, Vol. VI, trans. and annotated W. Montgomery Watt and M. V. McDonald (Albany, New York: State University of New York Press, 1988), p. 82. Chusroes (Chosroes) was the King of Persia, and the name Caesar referred to Heraclius, the Byzantine Emperor.

[31]  *The Meaning of the Glorious Koran*, p. 548.

[32]  *Tafsir Ibn Kathir*, Vol. 9, pp. 305-307; *Tafsir Ahsanul-Bayan*, Vol. 5, pp. 270-272; *Tafsir Ibn 'Abbas*, p. 714; and Jalalu'd-Din al-Mahalli and Jalalu'd-Din as-Suyuti, *Tafsir Al-Jalalayn*, trans. Aisha Bewley (London: Dar Al Taqwa Ltd., 2007), p. 1136.

Muhammad reiterated this idea that he spoke for Allah:

> *It was narrated that 'Abdullah bin 'Amr said: "I used to write down everything that I heard from the Messenger of Allah, wanting to memorize it, but the Quraish[33] told me not to do that, and said: 'Do you write down everything you hear from him? The Messenger of Allah is human, and speaks when he is angry, and when he is content.' So I stopped writing things down. I mentioned that to the Messenger of Allah, and he pointed to his mouth with his finger and said: 'Write, for by the One in Whose Hand is my soul, nothing comes out of it but the truth.'"[34]*

## 614

During the latter part of the Early Meccan Period, Muhammad's teachings that there was only one god were upsetting the Quraysh. The major reason was that in Mecca there was a building known at the Ka'bah. There were over 300 images of tribal gods inside this building, and the Arab tribes would make pilgrimages to Mecca to worship their respective gods. Providing housing for and feeding these pilgrims provided a lucrative income for the Meccans, which could be adversely affected if the people accepted the idea that there was only one god.

Consequently, leaders of the Quraysh made protests to Abu Talib, Muhammad's uncle and protector. Abu Talib sent for Muhammad:

> *Abu Talib said to him, "Nephew, how is it that your tribe are complaining of you and claiming that you are reviling their gods and saying this, that, and the other?"...the Messenger of God spoke and said, "Uncle, I want them to*

---

[33]    The Quraish (Quraysh) were the ruling non-Muslim tribe in Mecca.

[34]    *Sunan Abu Dawud*, Vol. 4, No. 3646, pp. 209-210. This *hadith* was also reported in *Tafsir Ibn Kathir*, Vol. 9, p. 307.

*utter one saying. If they say it, the Arabs will submit to them and the non-Arabs will pay the jizyah to them"..."There is no deity but God."*[35]

---

[35]     *The History of al-Tabari: Muhammad at Mecca*, p. 96. Ibn Ishaq reported that this happened later in 619, just prior to Abu Talib's death, and in ibn Ishaq's report Muhammad stated:

> *...you may give me one word by which you can rule the Arabs and subject the Persians to you...You must say There is no God but Allah and you must repudiate what you worship beside him.*

Muhammad ibn Ishaq, *The Life of Muhammad (Sirat Rasul Allah)*, trans. Alfred Guillaume (Karachi, Pakistan: Oxford University Press, 2007), pp. 191-192.

The time period of 619 was repeated in a modern biography of Muhammad where it was reported that Muhammad said to Abu Talib:

> *"I ask them only one thing. And if they accept this thing, the whole of Arabia will be under their control, and the non-Arabs will pay them tribute"..."There is no deity except the One God, Allah."*

Safiur Rahman Mubarakpuri, *When the Moon Split* (Riyadh, Kingdom of Saudi Arabia: Darussalam, 2009), p. 124.

This date was implied by ibn 'Abbas, who said that Abu Talib had fallen sick. When Muhammad came to him, Abu Talib said:

> *Why are your people complaining about you?  He* [Muhammad] *said: "O uncle, I want them to affirm one word by means of which the Arabs will submit to them and the non-Arabs will pay the jizyah to them."  He said: What is that?  He* [Muhammad] *said: "La ilaha illallah* [There is no god but Allah]. *"*

*Musnad Imam Ahmad Bin Hanbal*, Vol. 2, No. 2008, p. 288.  However, al-Tabari and ibn Sa'd (see footnote below) agreed that this particular event happened around 614, and I have used that date.

Ibn Sa'd reported a slightly different version of Muhammad's statement to Abu Talib:

> *The Apostle of Allah, may Allah bless him, said: Will you like to pledge your word to me, if I give this to you.* [sic] *By that word you will overpower Arabia and the part of Persia that adjoins it…Say: There is no god but Allah.*[36]

It is interesting to realize that within the first five years of Islam Muhammad was already establishing not only that he spoke for Allah, but that there was a militant component to Islam: non-Muslims were to be overpowered and either submit to Islam by becoming Muslims, or by paying the *Jizyah*.


## Middle Meccan Period (circa 615-619)

The development of the idea of a militant Islam continued with the "revelation" of this verse: [37]

Chapter 21, Verse 109

> *But if they (disbelievers, idolaters, Jews, Christians, polytheists) turn away (from Islamic Monotheism) say (to them O Muhammad): "I give you notice (of war as) to be known to us all alike. And I know not whether that which you are promised (i.e. the torment or the Day of Resurrection) is near or far."*

Ibn Kathir pointed out the hostility toward non-Muslims found in this verse:

---

[36]    *Kitab al-Tabaqat al-Kabir*, Vol. 1, p. 234. Ibn Sa'd agreed with al-Tabari and indicated that this event occurred around 614.

[37]    Pickthall stated that Chapter 21 belonged to the Middle Meccan Period - see *The Meaning of the Glorious Koran*, p. 328.

*(But if they turn away)* means, if they ignore that to which you call them. *(say: "I give you a notice to be known to us all alike…")* meaning, 'I declare that I am in a state of war with you as you are in a state of war with me. I have nothing to do with you just as you have nothing to do with me. [38]

This meaning was reiterated in two other *tafsirs*:

The *Tafsir Ahsanul-Bayan*:

*That is, just as I know that you are my enemy because you have turned away from the worship of One God, so should you also know that I am your enemy. We are at war with each other. The "promise" here means the promised Day of Resurrection, or Allah's promise to the Muslims that He will give them victory over the non-Muslims, or Allah's promise that He will give His Messenger leave to wage war against the disbelievers. [39]*

The *Tafsir Al-Jalalayn*:

**If they turn their backs** *on that,* **then say: 'I have informed all of you equally** *– of a war which will be waged against you…* [40]

It is interesting that in *The Noble Qur'an* the footnote for this verse states, "See the footnote of (V. 2:193)." [41] Here is that footnote for 2:193:

---

[38]     *Tafsir Ibn Kathir*, Vol. 6, p. 513.

[39]     *Tafsir Ahsanul-Bayan*, Vol. 3, p. 554.

[40]     *Tafsir Al-Jalalayn*, p. 707.

[41]     *Interpretation of the Meanings of The Noble Qur'an* [*The Noble Qur'an*], trans. Muhammad Muhsin Khan and Muhammad Taqi-ud-Din Al-Hilali (Riyadh, Kingdom of Saudi Arabia: Darussalam, 2007), n. 1, p. 445.

*Narrated Ibn 'Umar: Allah's Messenger said, "I have
been ordered (by Allah) to fight against the people till they
testify that...(none has the right to be worshipped but
Allah and that Muhammad is the Messenger of Allah), and
perform As-Salat (the prayers) and give Zakat (obligatory
charity), so if they perform all that, then they save their
lives and properties from me...* [42]

So by the end of the Middle Meccan Period, not only was Muhammad
talking about a militant Islam, but there was a verse of the Koran telling
Muslims that they were in a state of war against non-Muslims who rejected
Islam.


## Late Meccan Period (circa 619-622)

Beginning around 614 and continuing up until his emigration to Medina in
September 622, Muhammad had made it a regular practice to approach the
members of Arab tribes coming to Mecca during the pilgrimage season.
Here is how Muhammad would appeal to them to convert to Islam:

*...he approached each tribe in its halting place saying: O
people! say there is no god but Allah; you will prosper
and become masters of Arabia, and the Persians will
surrender before you in humiliation, and if you believe
you will become kings in paradise.* [43]

It was also reported that Muhammad would say to the Arab tribes:

*O people! Say: "La Ilaha Illallah" (none has the right to
be worshipped except Allah) and you will be successful
and you will rule over the Arabs thereby and the non-*

---

[42]     Ibid., n. 3A, p. 51.

[43]     *Kitab al-Tabaqat al-Kabir*, Vol. 1, p. 250.

23

*Arabs will submit to you; and if you die you will be kings in Paradise.*[44]

So Muhammad's appeal for conversion to Islam was a militant appeal, based on the claim that by doing so the converts would rule over Arabia and the non-Arabs would "surrender" and "submit" to them.

The idea of non-Muslims submitting to the Muslims and to Islam was emphasized in two verses of the Koran "revealed" during this time period. [45] Here is the first verse:

---

[44]     Muhammad ibn 'Abdul Wahhab at-Tamimi, *Abridged Biography of Prophet Muhammad*, ed. 'Abdur-Rahman bin Nasir Al-Barrak, 'Abdul 'Azeez bin 'Abdullah Ar-Rajihi, and Muhammad Al-'Ali Al-Barrak (Riyadh, Kingdom of Saudi Arabia: Darussalam, 2003), p. 117.

[45]     Ibn Kathir wrote that Chapter 13 was a Meccan chapter - see *Tafsir Ibn Kathir*, Vol. 5, p. 230. The *Tafsir Al-Jalalayn*, p. 521, and the *Tafsir Ibn 'Abbas*, p. 301, stated that Chapter 13 was a Meccan chapter except for Verses 31 and 43 (Verse 31 was erroneously referred to as Verse 32 in the *Tafsir Al-Jalalayn*); but the *Tafsir Al-Jalalayn* also stated that it was possible that this was a Medinan chapter, except for Verses 32-33, which were Meccan. The entire chapter was considered to be Medinan in 'Abd ar-Rahman b. Nasir as-Sa'di, *Tafsir As-Sa'di*, trans. S. Abd al-Hamid (Floral Park, New York: The Islamic Literary Foundation: 2014), Vol. 2, p. 343.

Pickthall made the argument that Chapter 13, and 13:15 and 13:41, were Meccan:

> *According to some ancient authorities, it is a Meccan Surah* [Chapter] *with the exception of two verses revealed at Al-Madinah; according to others, a Madinan Surah, with the exception of two verses revealed at Mecca. The very fact of such wholesale difference of opinion favours the Meccan attribution because there could be no such doubt about a complete Madinan Surah, owing to the great number of witnesses...* [this Chapter is] *A late Meccan Surah for the most part.*

*The Meaning of the Glorious Koran*, p. 248.

Chapter 13, Verse 41

> *See they not that We gradually reduce the land (of the disbelievers, by giving it to the believers, in war victories) from its outlying borders. And Allah judges, there is none to put back His Judgement and He is Swift at reckoning.*

This verse was understood to mean that the Muslims would gain domination over the land of the non-Muslims.[46]

The second verse stated that all would prostrate themselves before Allah, "willingly or unwillingly":

Chapter 13, Verse 15

> *And to Allah (Alone) falls in prostration whoever is in the heavens and the earth, willingly or unwillingly, and so do their shadows in the mornings and in the afternoons.*

This verse was discussed in the *Tafsir Ibn Kathir*:

> *Allah affirms His might and power, for He has full control over everything, and everything is subservient to Him. Therefore, everything, including the believers, prostrate to Allah willingly, while the disbelievers do so unwillingly.*[47]

The *Tafsir Ahsanul-Bayan* explained:

> *The verse expresses the might and majesty of Allah...All things, even their shadows, lie prostrate before him, willingly or unwillingly.*[48]

---

[46]     *Tafsir As-Sa'di*, Vol. 2, p. 365; *Tafsir Ibn Kathir*, Vol. 5, p. 302; and *Tafsir Ahsanul-Bayan*, Vol. 3, p. 110.

[47]     *Tafsir Ibn Kathir*, Vol. 5, p. 256.

[48]     *Tafsir Ahsanul-Bayan*, Vol. 3, p. 89.

The fact that all would submit to Allah, even unwillingly, was noted in three other *tafsirs*:

*Tafsir Ibn 'Abbas*:

> *...it is also said that (willingly) refers to those who were born Muslim while (unwillingly) refers to those who were coerced to embrace Islam...*[49]

*Tafsir Al-Jalalayn*:

> **Everyone in heaven and earth prostrates to Allah, willingly** – *referring to the believers* – **or unwillingly** – *referring to the hypocrites and those who are compelled to do so by the sword,* **as do their shadows in the morning and the evening.**[50]

*Tafsir As-Sa'di*:

> *All thing* [sic] *in the heavens and the earth submit to Allah, and prostrate themselves before Him,* **willingly or unwillingly.**[51]

So even before the Muslims left Mecca for Medina, they were being taught that everything would have to submit to them and their god Allah, whether willingly or unwillingly.

During this time period the Muslims were also being reminded to obey Allah and obey Muhammad, and that the "fire of Hell" was waiting for those who disobeyed (64:12[52] and 72:32,[53] respectively).

---

[49]    *Tafsir Ibn 'Abbas*, p. 304.

[50]    *Tafsir Al-Jalalayn*, p. 526.

[51]    *Tafsir As-Sa'di*, Vol. 2, p. 351.

And during Muhammad's last year in Mecca (621-622), [54] Muslims were ordered by Allah to specifically follow what Muhammad said, for Muhammad commanded all that was lawful and forbade all that was forbidden:

Chapter 7, Verse 157

> *Those who follow the Messenger...he commands them for Al-Mar'uf (...all that Islam has ordained); and forbids them from Al-Munkar (...all that Islam has forbidden)...*

The *Tafsir Ahsanul-Bayan* summed this verse up:

> *This verse is clear textual evidence (nass) which proves beyond doubt that deliverance in the Hereafter is impossible without a firm belief in the Prophetic mission of Muhammad, and faith is not acceptable to Allah unless it conforms to how the Messenger of Allah, defined it. The verse negates the concept of so-called "Unity of Faiths."* [55]

So Muslims were not only to believe in Muhammad, but their "faith" would not be acceptable to Allah unless it conformed to how Muhammad "defined it."

---

[52]    Chapter 64 was "generally regarded" as a Late Meccan chapter – see *The Meaning of the Glorious Koran*, p. 588.

[53]    Chapter 72 was also a Late Meccan chapter – see *The Meaning of the Glorious Koran*, p. 613.

[54]    Chapter 7 was "revealed" during this time period – see *The Meaning of the Glorious Koran*, p. 157.

[55]    *Tafsir Ahsanul-Bayan*, Vol. 2, p. 231.

## September 622

Shortly before Muhammad left Mecca to emigrate to Medina, a group of non-Muslim Meccans were gathered outside Muhammad's front door. During the encounter with this group, Muhammad confirmed that if they became Muslims they would be the "kings of the Arabs and the non-Arabs," but if they did not become Muslims they would "meet with slaughter from him":

> ...among them [the Meccans] was Abu Jahl b. Hisham, who said, while they were waiting at his door, "Muhammad claims that if you follow him in his religion, you shall be the kings of the Arabs and the non-Arabs, that after your death you shall be brought back to life and your lot shall then be gardens like the gardens of Jordan. He also claims that if you do not do this, you shall meet with slaughter from him, and that after your death you shall be brought back to life, and your lot shall then be a fire, in which you shall burn." Then the Messenger of God came out, took a handful of dust and said, "Yes, I do say that; and you are one of them."[56]

---

[56]     *The History of al-Tabari: Muhammad at Mecca*, p. 143.

This was similarly reported in *The Life of Muhammad (Sirat Rasul Allah)*, p. 222:

> ...when they were all outside his door Abu Jahl said to them: 'Muhammad alleges that if you follow him you will be kings of the Arabs and the Persians. Then after death you will be raised to gardens like those of the Jordan. But if you do not follow him you will be slaughtered, and when you are raised from the dead you will be burned in the fire of hell.' The apostle came out to them with a handful of dust saying: 'I do say that. You are one of them.'

However, it is interesting to note that when this incident was reported in a 20th century, award-winning biography of Muhammad, it was stated that Abu Jahl was "mocking" Muhammad, and there was no confirming response from Muhammad:

So we can see that just before he emigrated to Medina, Muhammad was still telling non-Muslims that if they became Muslims they would rule over the non-Muslims, but now, if they refused to convert they would "meet with slaughter from him."

The Meccan period lasted from 610-622. It was during this time that the religion of Islam began and its fundamental doctrines were being established. As we have seen, by the end of this period, it had already been established that:

1. Muslims were to obey Allah, and specifically Muhammad.

2. Muhammad spoke for Allah and commanded what was made permissible by Allah, and forbade what was forbidden by Allah.

3. There was a militant component to Islam:

    a. Those who converted to Islam would rule over non-Muslims and be in a state of hostility toward them;

    b. The non-Muslims would have to submit to Allah and Islam, willingly or unwillingly;

    c. And now there was the threat of "slaughter" for those who refused to become Muslims.

---

*Abu Jahl, the great enemy of Islam, used to walk about proudly and arrogantly mocking at Muhammad's words, saying to the people around him: "Muhammad claims that if you follow him, he will appoint you rulers over the Arabs and non-Arabs and in the Hereafter your reward will be Gardens similar to those in Jordan, otherwise he will slaughter you, and after death you will be burnt in fire."*

*The Sealed Nectar*, p. 204.

# 5

# The Early Medinan Period (622-627)

In the summer of 622 Muhammad said that he had received permission from Allah for the Muslims to start leaving an increasingly hostile Mecca and settle in the town of Medina, which had a small, but growing, Muslim community. Muhammad himself followed in September of 622. Did the commands of Allah or the teachings of Muhammad change?

Right after Muhammad arrived in Medina, a verse of the Koran was "revealed" that threatened Jews and Christians with punishment if they did not believe in Islam:[57]

Chapter 4, Verse 47

> *O you who have been given the Scripture (Jews and Christians)! Believe in what We have revealed (to Muhammad) confirming what is (already) with you, before we efface faces (by making them look like the back of necks; without nose, mouth and eyes) and turn them hindwards, or curse them as We cursed the Sabbath-breakers. And the Commandment of Allah is always executed.*

---

[57]     I established the time frame for this "revelation" based on the following reports: 1) 'Abdullah ibn Salam became a Muslim after the "revelation" of this verse – see *Tafsir Al-Jalalayn*, p. 193, and *Tafsir Ibn 'Abbas*, p. 108; and 2) 'Abdullah ibn Salam became a Muslim when Muhammad arrived in Medina – see *The Life of Muhammad (Sirat Rasul Allah)*, pp. 240-241; *The Sealed Nectar*, p. 225; and Sa'd Yusuf Abu 'Aziz, *Men and Women Around the Messenger*, trans. Suleman Fulani (Riyadh, Kingdom of Saudi Arabia: Darussalam, 2009), p. 489.

Ibn Kathir explained that Allah was ordering the Jews and Christians to believe in Islam. If they failed to do so, they would be punished for ignoring the truth of Islam:

> *Allah commands the People of the Scriptures to believe in what He has sent down to His servant and Messenger, Muhammad, the Glorious Book...(before We efface faces and turn them backwards).*[58]

The *Tafsir Al-Jalalayn* stated that this verse was

> *a conditional threat and that when some of them became Muslim that threat was removed.*[59]

The *Tafsir as-Sa'di* also explained this as a threat:

> *Allah commands the Jews and the Christians to embrace faith in Prophet Muhammad and in the Noble Qur'an that was revealed to him...**before We obliterate faces and turn them backwards**. This is a recompense for their offense* [of not converting to Islam].[60]

And the footnote for this verse in *The Noble Qur'an* stated:

> *This Verse is a severe warning to the Jews and Christians, and an absolute obligation that they must believe in Allah's Messenger Muhammad and in his Message of Islamic Monotheism and in this Qur'an.*[61]

---

[58]    *Tafsir Ibn Kathir*, Vol. 2, p. 479.

[59]    *Tafsir Al-Jalalayn*, p. 193.

[60]    'Abd ar-Rahman b. Nasir as-Sa'di, *Tafsir As-Sa'di*, trans. S. Abd al-Hamid (Floral Park, New York: The Islamic Literary Foundation: 2012), Vol. 1, pp. 373-374.

[61]    *The Noble Qur'an*, n. 1, p. 129. Muhammad later repeated this warning:

So Muhammad had just arrived in Medina and already Jews and Christians were being warned about the dire consequences of not converting to Islam.

## May 623 – The Command for *Jihad*[62]

Approximately eight months after Muhammad emigrated to Medina, he received a "revelation" that commanded Muslims to fight non-Muslims. This verse was first "revealed" in May 623, and then "revealed" again in December 623:[63]

---

*It is narrated on the authority of Abu Huraira that the Messenger of Allah (SAW) said: By Him in whose hand is the life of Muhammad, he who amongst the community of Jews or Christians hears about me but does not affirm his belief in that with which I have been sent and dies in this state (of disbelief), he shall be but one of the denizens of Hell-Fire.*

Abu'l Hussain 'Asakir-ud-Din Muslim bin Hajjaj al-Qushayri al-Naisaburi, *Sahih Muslim*, trans. 'Abdul Hamid Siddiqi (New Delhi, India: Adam Publishers and Distributors, 2008), Vol. 1, No. 153, p. 103.

[62]     *Al-Jihad (holy fighting) in Allah's Cause (with full force of numbers and weaponry) is given the utmost importance in Islam and is one of its pillars (on which it stands). By Jihad Islam is established, Allah's Word is made superior, (His Word being La ilaha illallah which means none has the right to be worshipped but Allah), and His religion (Islam) is propagated. By abandoning Jihad (may Allah protect us from that) Islam is destroyed and the Muslims fall into an inferior position; their honour is lost, their lands are stolen, their rule and authority vanish. Jihad is an obligatory duty in Islam on every Muslim, and he who tries to escape from this duty, or does not in his innermost heart wish to fulfil [sic] this duty, dies with one of the qualities of a hypocrite.*

*The Noble Qur'an*, n. 1, p. 50. This footnote in *The Noble Qur'an* was used to explain the meaning of the first part of 2:190: *And fight in the way of Allah...*

[63]     *Tafsir Ibn 'Abbas*, p. 44. Ibn 'Abbas stated that this verse was first

        *revealed about Sa'd Ibn Abi Waqqas, al-Miqdad Ibn al-Aswad and their associates.*

Chapter 2, Verse 216

> *Jihad (holy fighting in Allah's Cause) is ordained for you*
> *(Muslims) though you dislike it, and it may be that you*
> *dislike a thing which is good for you and that you like a*
> *thing which is bad for you. Allah knows but you do not*
> *know.*

The *Tafsir as-Sa'di* explained this verse:

> *This noble verse made fighting in the cause of Allah*
> *mandatory upon the faithful. Previously, they were*
> *ordered to refrain from fighting because they were weak*
> *and could not bear the burden. When the Prophet*
> *migrated to Madinah, the Muslims grew in number and*
> *became stronger, so Allah gave them the commandment to*
> *fight.*[64]

According to the *Tafsir Al-Qurtubi*, this verse made it obligatory for the
Muslims to fight non-Muslims:

> *This means that fighting is obligatory and refers to the*
> *obligation of jihad...The Prophet, may Allah bless him and*

---

This appears to refer to the expedition of Sa'd ibn Abi Waqqas to Al-Kharrar in
May 623. During this expedition, the banner was carried by al-Miqdad b. 'Amr
(see Abu Ja'far Muhammad b. Jarir al-Tabari, *The History of al-Tabari: The
Foundation of the Community*, Vol. VII, trans. and annotated W. Montgomery
Watt and M. V. McDonald (Albany, New York: State University of New York
Press, 1987), p. 11).

Al-Miqdad b. 'Amr was also known as Al-Miqdad ibn al-Aswad; see the "Index"
entry for Al-Miqdad b. 'Amr in Muhammad b. 'Umar al-Waqidi, *The Life of
Muhammad: Al-Waqidi's Kitab al-Maghazi*, trans. Rizwi Faizer, Amal Ismail, and
AbdulKader Tayob, ed. Rizwi Faizer (London and New York: Routledge, 2013),
p. 560.

[64]     *Tafsir as-Sa'di*, Vol. 1, pp. 152-153.

*grant him peace, was not given permission to fight while he was in Makka. When he emigrated, he was given permission to fight those idolaters who fought him and then he was given permission to fight idolaters in general.*[65]

This was reiterated in the *Tafsir Al-Jalalayn*:

**Fighting** *against the unbelievers* **is prescribed** *and hereby made obligatory* **for you even if it is hateful to you***...* [66]

Ibn Kathir noted that this verse "made it obligatory for the Muslims to fight in *Jihad* against the evil of the enemy who transgress against Islam"; he stated that this verse was "general in meaning."[67]

What does it mean to "fight in Allah's Cause"? Muhammad provided this explanation:

*Narrated Abu Musa: A man came to the Prophet and asked, "O Allah's Messenger! What kind of fighting is in Allah's Cause? (I ask this), for some of us fight because of being enraged and angry and some for the sake of their pride and haughtiness." The Prophet raised his head (as the questioner was standing) and said, "He who fights that Allah's Word (i.e. Allah's Religion of Islamic Monotheism) should be superior, fights in Allah's Cause.*"[68]

---

[65]     *Tafsir Al-Qurtubi*, p. 544.

[66]     *Tafsir Al-Jalalayn*, p. 79.

[67]     *Tafsir Ibn Kathir*, Vol. 1, pp. 596-597.

[68]     *Sahih Al-Bukhari*, Vol. 1, Book 3, No. 123, p. 128. This *hadith*, with similar wording, was also reported in *Sahih Muslim*, Vol. 6, No. 1904, p. 286.

34

So approximately eight months after the Muslims had emigrated to Medina, Allah was commanding them to fight non-Muslims so Islam would be superior.

## February 624 – The Doctrine of Abrogation

As indicated in the earlier chapter about the Doctrine of Abrogation, the basis for this doctrine was 2:106 of the Koran. This verse was "revealed" in response to criticism from non-Muslims when the direction in which Muslims were required to pray (the *qiblah*) was changed from Jerusalem to Mecca around February 624.[69]

Muslim scholars considered the changing of the *qiblah* to be the first instance of abrogation in the Koran.[70]

## March 624 – Fight Until There is Only Islam

In this month the first major battle occurred between the Muslims and a large Meccan force: the Battle of Badr. Before the battle started Muhammad reminded the Muslim warriors that he spoke for Allah:

> *As for that which is after, indeed I urge you to what God urges you, and I forbid you from what God forbids you.*[71]

The Muslims won this battle, reinforcing the militant aspect of Islam and consequently adding new Muslims to the fold:

---

[69]     *Tafsir Al-Qurtubi*, p. 321; and *Abridged Biography of Prophet Muhammad*, p. 188.

[70]     *Tafsir Al-Qurtubi*, p. 382; and *Tafsir Ibn Kathir*, Vol. 1, p. 429.

[71]     *The Life of Muhammad: Al-Waqidi's Kitab al-Maghazi*, p. 31.

*The sight of the triumphant Muslims entering Madinah*
*with dozens of captives led many people to become*
*Muslim.*[72]

And Muhammad was henceforth to be considered in a "new dimension":

*The Prophet now entered Madinah as a man to be counted*
*for in a new dimension – the military field. In*
*consequence, a large number of the people of Madinah*
*embraced Islam, which added a lot to the strength, power*
*and moral standing of the true religion.*[73]

After the Battle of Badr, Chapter 8 of the Koran was "revealed" about that battle.[74] In this chapter we find a number of verses in which Allah commands the Muslims to obey both him and Muhammad (e.g. 8:1, 8:13, and 8:46).

And there was one verse in particular that focused on obeying Muhammad:

Chapter 8, Verse 20

*O you who believe! Obey Allah and His Messenger, and*
*turn not away from him (i.e. Messenger Muhammad)*
*while you are hearing.*

---

[72]     *When the Moon Split*, p. 201.

[73]     *The Sealed Nectar*, p. 275.

[74]     *Tafsir Ibn Kathir*, Vol. 4, p. 252; *The Life of Muhammad (Sirat Rasul Allah)*, p. 321; *Sahih Muslim*, Vol. 8, No. 3031, p. 404; and 'Imaduddeen Isma'eel ibn Katheer al-Qurashi, *In Defence of the True Faith: Battles, Expeditions, Peace Treaties and their Consequences in the life of Prophet Muhammad*, trans. Research Department of Darussalam (Riyadh, Kingdom of Saudi Arabia: Darussalam, 2010), p. 62.

The *Tafsir Ibn Kathir* explained this verse:

> *Allah commands His believing servants to obey Him and
> His Messenger and warns them against defying him
> [Muhammad] ...Allah said, ...neither refrain from obeying
> him or following his commands nor indulge in what he
> forbade...*[75]

Ibn Ishaq pointed out that this verse meant:

> *Do not contradict his [Muhammad's] orders when you
> hear him speak and while you assert that you are on his
> side.*[76]

And at this time we also find a command from Allah specifically ordering
the Muslims to fight non-Muslims until Islam was the only religion:

Chapter 8, Verse 39

> *And fight them until there is no more Fitnah (disbelief and
> polytheism, i.e. worshipping others besides Allah), and the
> religion (worship) will all be for Allah Alone (in the whole
> of the world). But if they cease (worshipping others
> besides Allah), then certainly, Allah is All-Seer of what
> they do.*

---

[75]     *Tafsir Ibn Kathir*, Vol. 4, pp. 283-284.  As Muhammad himself said:

> *Al-Miqdam bin Ma'dikarib narrated that the Messenger of
> Allah said: "...whatever the Messenger of Allah made unlawful,
> it is the same as what Allah made unlawful."*

*Jami' At-Tirmidhi*, Vol. 5, No. 2664, pp. 63-64.

[76]     *The Life of Muhammad (Sirat Rasul Allah)*, p. 322.

This message was clearly presented in our *tafsirs*:

The *Tafsir Al-Jalalayn* stated:

> **Fight them until there is no more fitna (shirk)**[77] **and the din is Allah's along** – *meaning that only He is worshipped.*[78]

The *Tafsir Ibn Kathir*, in a section titled *The Order to fight to eradicate Shirk and Kufr*, pointed out:

> *...(and the religion will all be for Allah alone) "So that there is no more Kufr (disbelief)...The Messenger of Allah said, I was commanded to fight against the people until they proclaim, 'There is no deity worthy of worship except Allah.' If and when they say it, they will preserve their blood and wealth from me...*[79]

The *Tafsir Ahsanul-Bayan*:

> *Here fitnah (affliction) means disbelief or paganism, or the power of disbelievers and pagans...continue fighting until you put an end to the power of disbelievers. Until Allah alone is worshipped in the entire world.*[80]

---

[77]     *Shirk*: polytheism, worshipping others along with Allah, and/or ascribing partners to Allah (including ascribing a Son to him). *Shirk* is the one unforgiveable sin in Islam (4:48 and 4:116). By believing that Jesus is the Son of God, Christians commit *Shirk*.

[78]     *Tafsir Al-Jalalayn*, p. 385.

[79]     *Tafsir Ibn Kathir*, Vol. 4, p. 315.

[80]     *Tafsir Ahsanul-Bayan*, Vol. 2, p. 293.

The *Tafsir as-Sa'di*:

> *Concerning the address that was made towards the*
> *believers about the commandment concerning their*
> *attitude and dealings with the disbelievers, Allah says to*
> *them,* ***fight them until there is no more oppression****, that*
> *is, [fight against] the polytheists who stop people from the*
> *path of Allah until they declare submission to the*
> *commandments of Islam,* ***and all worship is for Allah***
> ***alone****. This is the only purpose of waging jihad and*
> *fighting the enemies of Islam...His religion, for which the*
> *entire universe has been created, is protected until it*
> *becomes dominant over all other religions.*[81]

And after the Battle of Badr, Muhammad stated that he had been "helped by fear" on the part of his enemy. [82]

But this "fear" did not seem to extend to the first of the Jewish tribes in Medina that Muhammad attacked.

---

[81]     *Tafsir as-Sa'di*, Vol. 2, p. 105.

[82]     *The Life of Muhammad (Sirat Rasul Allah)*, p. 326.  Here is a *hadith* that expanded on this idea:

> *It was narrated that Jabir bin 'Abdullah said: "The Messenger*
> *of Allah said: 'I have been given five things that were not given*
> *to anyone before me: I have been supported with fear being*
> *struck into the hearts of my enemy for a distance of one month's*
> *travel...*

Abu 'Abdur-Rahman Ahmad bin Shu'aib bin 'Ali bin Sinan bin Bahr An-Nasa'i, *Sunan An-Nasa'i*, trans. Nasiruddin al-Khattab (Riyadh, Kingdom of Saudi Arabia: Darussalam, 2007), Vol. 1, No. 432, p. 254.

# April 624 – O Jews!  Accept Islam or Else

After the defeat of the Meccans at the Battle of Badr, Muhammad turned his attention to the Banu Qaynuqa, one of the Jewish tribes in Medina. Muhammad called for these Jews to convert to Islam; if they refused, he threatened them with the same punishment the Muslims had inflicted on the Meccans.

Let's see how five authoritative biographies of Muhammad reported this matter:

## The Life of Muhammad (Sirat Rasul Allah)

> *When God smote Quraysh at Badr, the apostle assembled the Jews in the market of the B. Qaynuqa when he came to Medina and called on them to accept Islam before God should treat them as he had treated Quraysh. They answered, 'Don't deceive yourself, Muhammad. You have killed a number of inexperienced Quraysh who did not know how to fight. But if you fight us you will learn that we are men and that you have met your equal.* [83]

## In Defence of the True Faith: Battles, Expeditions, Peace Treaties and their Consequences in the life of Prophet Muhammad

> *...Allah's Messenger, peace be upon him, requested them to gather in their marketplace and he addressed them saying: "O company of Jews, be careful of the kind of tragedy that befell the Quraish, accept Islam for you have come to know that I am a Prophet that has been sent...They replied: "O Muhammad, do you assume that*

---

[83]     *The Life of Muhammad (Sirat Rasul Allah)*, p. 260.  A similar narration was made by ibn 'Abbas: Muhammad assembled the Jews in the market place and said, "O Jews, become Muslim before there befalls you something like that which befell the Quraish."  See *Sunan Abu Dawud*, Vol. 3, No. 3001, p. 498.

*we are your people? Do not be deceived by the fact that
you fought with a group who lack the knowledge of
military tactics and you scored an opportunity. If you
fight us then you will know what sort of people we are (in
military capability).*[84]

## The History of al-Tabari: The Foundation of the Community

*What happened with regard to the Banu Qaynuqa' was
that the Messenger of God assembled them in the Market
of the Banu Qaynuqa' and said, "O Jews, beware lest God
bring on you the like of the retribution which he brought
on Quraysh. Accept Islam, for you know that I am a
prophet sent by God."...They replied, "Muhammad, do
you think that we are like your people? Do not be deluded
by the fact that you met a people with no knowledge of
war...By God, if you fight us you will know that we are
real men!"*[85]

## The Sealed Nectar

*When Allah's Messenger defeated the Quraish at Badr
and returned to Madinah, he gathered the Jews at the
bazaar of Banu Qainuqa'. He then said: "O you Jews!
Enter Islam before you suffer what happened to the
Quraish." They replied: "O Muhammad! Do not deceive
yourself, you merely fought a party of the Quraish who
were inexperienced at war. But if you want to fight us*

---

[84]    *In Defence of the True Faith: Battles, Expeditions, Peace Treaties and
their Consequences in the life of Prophet Muhammad*, p. 87.

[85]    *The History of al-Tabari: The Foundation of the Community*, p. 85.

*then know that we are an entire people! And indeed you
have not met up with anyone like us before!"*[86]

<u>*The Life of Muhammad: Al-Waqidi's Kitab al-Maghazi*</u>

*When the Prophet overcame the companions of Badr and
arrived in Medina, the Jews acted wrongfully and
destroyed the agreement that was between them and the
Messenger of God. The Prophet sent for them and having
gathered them together, said, "O Jewish people, submit,
for, by God, you surely know that I am the Messenger of
God, before God inflicts upon you the like of what he
inflicted on the Quraysh." The Jews said, "O
Muhammad, let not those whom you met deceive you.
Surely you have defeated a people who have no
experience in war. But we are, by God, the masters of
war, and if you fight us you will learn that you have not
fought with the likes of us."*[87]

So in April 624 we have our first clear incident in which Muhammad
himself gave a tribe of non-Muslims the choice of converting to Islam or
fighting the Muslims. The Jews of Banu Qaynuqa refused to convert and
the Muslims besieged them. After 15 days the Jews surrendered, they
were expelled from Medina, and their property was divided among the
Muslims.

It is interesting to note that after the Banu Qaynuqa were defeated
Muhammad had originally wanted to kill his fettered captives. But he was
persuaded otherwise by 'Adbullah b. Ubayy, who went to the point of
grabbing Muhammad by the collar to get him to exile the Banu Qaynuqa
instead of killing them. Muhammad finally had this to say about the Banu

---

[86]     *The Sealed Nectar*, pp. 283-284.

[87]     *The Life of Muhammad: Al-Waqidi's Kitab al-Maghazi*, pp. 87-88.

Qaynuqa: "Let them go; may God curse them, and may he curse [b. Ubayy] with them."[88]


## June 24, 624 – June 1, 626 (3 AH–4 AH)

Chapter 3 of the Koran was "revealed" during this time period.[89] Among the verses in this chapter are a number that reiterate the importance of obeying Muhammad.

In 3:31 we find that the proof of a Muslim's love for Allah is to be found in the extent to which that Muslim follows the teachings and commands of Muhammad (similar to 7:157, "revealed" in 621-622):

> *Say (O Muhammad to mankind): "If you (really) love Allah, then follow me (i.e. accept Islamic Monotheism, follow the Qur'an and the Sunnah), Allah will love you and forgive you your sins. And Allah is Oft-Forgiving, Most Merciful.*

The *Tafsir Ibn Kathir*, in a section titled *Allah's Love is Attained by Following the Messenger*, explained:

> *This honorable Ayah* [verse] *judges against those who claim to love Allah, yet do not follow the way of Muhammad. Such people are not true in their claim until they follow the Shari'ah (Law) of Muhammad and his religion in all his statements, actions and conditions.*[90]

---

[88]    *The History of al-Tabari, The Foundation of the Community*, p. 86. This incident was also mentioned in *The Life of Muhammad (Sirat Rasul Allah)*, p. 363.

[89]    *The Meaning of the Glorious Koran*, p. 66.

[90]    *Tafsir Ibn Kathir*, Vol. 2, p. 145.

The *Tafsir as-Sa'di* provided a similar explanation:

> *If you claim to have love for Allah...this claim must be proven factually. The proof of its genuineness is the obedience of the Prophet at all times and in all circumstances...He who does not obey the Prophet will not obtain Allah's love...*[91]

As did the *Tafsir Ahsanul-Bayan*:

> *...for the only way to win divine pleasure is to believe in His Last Messenger and follow him. In other words, the criterion is Muhammad.*[92]

In 3:32 the command to obey Allah and Muhammad is clear-cut:

> *Say (O Muhammad): "Obey Allah and the Messenger (Muhammad)." But if they turn away, then Allah does not like the disbelievers."*

The *Tafsir Ahsanul-Bayan* explained this verse:

> *Again, in this verse, Allah tells us to follow the Messenger of Allah...salvation depends on following him* [Muhammad], *and that refusal to follow him is disbelief.*[93]

The *Tafsir As-Sa'di* went to the crux of this verse:

> *In this noble verse, Allah has conferred the most comprehensive commandment to His servants: obedience to Him and to His Prophet [Muhammad].*[94]

---

91      *Tafsir as-Sa'di*, Vol. 1, p. 234.

92      *Tafsir Ahsanul-Bayan*, Vol. 1, p. 291.

93      Ibid., p. 292.

And in these next two verses we find again that all creatures will submit to Allah, willingly or unwillingly, and that the only religion acceptable to Allah is Islam:

Chapter 3, Verse 83

> *Do they seek other than the religion of Allah (the true*
> *Islamic Monotheism worshipping none but Allah Alone),*
> *while to Him submitted all creatures in the heavens and*
> *the earth, willingly or unwillingly. And to Him shall they*
> *all be returned.*[95]

What do our *tafsirs* say about all creatures submitting to Allah "willingly or unwillingly" in this verse?

---

[94]     *Tafsir as-Sa'di*, Vol. 1, p. 235.

[95]     The *Tafsir Ibn 'Abbas* explained that this "revelation" came about because of a dispute between Christians and Jews:

> *Allah then mentions the dispute of the Jews and Christians and*
> *the question which they put to the Prophet (pbuh) regarding*
> *who really follows the religion of Abraham. When the Prophet*
> *(pbuh) told them that they were both far from the Religion of*
> *Abraham, they said that they did not accept this judgement* [and
> 3:83 was "revealed"].

*Tafsir Ibn 'Abbas*, p. 78. This story was similarly related in *Al-Wahidi's Asbab al-Nuzul*, p. 53. The reason both Jews and Christians are "far from the Religion of Abraham" is explained in 3:67 of the Koran:

> *Ibrahim (Abraham) was neither a Jew nor a Christian, but he*
> *was a true Muslim Hanifa (Islamic Monotheism – to worship*
> *none but Allah Alone) and he was not of Al-Mushrikun.*

*Mushrikun*: Polytheists, pagans, idolaters and disbelievers in the Oneness of Allah and His Messenger Muhammad; people who associate partners/a Son with Allah.

The *Tafsir Ibn Kathir*:

> *Therefore, the faithful believer submits to Allah in heart and body, while the disbeliever unwillingly submits to Him in body only...* [96]

The *Tafsir Ahsanul-Bayan*:

> *There is nothing in heavens or the earth which does not obey Allah. Everything is subject to His will and under His command. How, then, can you refuse to bow your head to Him and accept Islam?* [97]

The *Tafsir as-Sa'di*:

> *Some of them have voluntarily accepted Allah's obedience and willingly worship him... while others are involuntarily under His control, compelled to accept this submission.* [98]

This next verse plainly states that the only religion acceptable to Allah is Islam:

Chapter 3, Verse 85

> *And whoever seeks a religion other than Islam, it will never be accepted of him, and in the Hereafter he will be one of the losers.*

---

[96]     *Tafsir Ibn Kathir*, Vol. 2, p. 202.

[97]     *Tafsir Ahsanul-Bayan*, Vol. 1, p. 328.

[98]     *Tafsir as-Sa'di*, Vol. 1, p. 257.

Under the heading *The Only Valid Religion To Allah is Islam*, Ibn Kathir explained this verse meant that

> ...*whoever seeks other than what Allah has legislated, it will not be accepted from him.*[99]

The *Tafsir As-Sa'di* pointed out:

> *Allah has chosen the religion of Islam for his servants, so whoever follows another religion other than Allah's chosen religion, all his deeds will be rejected...Therefore, all other religions, except Islam, are mere falsehoods.*[100]

So during this time period we have Koran verses reiterating the importance of obeying Muhammad, stating that everything submits to Allah, willingly or unwillingly, and that Islam is the only religion acceptable to Allah.

Let's consider some incidents that occurred during this time period.


## November 624 – Convert or Be Killed: Furat Chooses

This incident happened after a Muslim military expedition to Al-Qarada. The purpose of this expedition was to intercept a wealthy Quraysh caravan. The caravan was intercepted and brought back to Muhammad for the division of the plunder. There was also one captive, Furat the caravan guide:

> *Furat Ibn Hayyan was captured and brought before the Prophet, may Allah bless him. He was asked to embrace Islam and then his life would be safe. He embraced Islam and the Apostle of Allah, may Allah bless him, saved him from being killed.*[101]

---

[99]    *Tafsir Ibn Kathir*, Vol. 2, p. 204.

[100]   *Tafsir as-Sa'di*, Vol. 1, p. 258.

[101]   *Kitab al-Tabaqat al-Kabir*, Vol. 2, p. 42.

It was also reported that the approach to Furat was more direct, simply offering him the choice of either converting to Islam or being killed:

> *Included among the prisoners was al-Furat b. Hayyan. He was brought before the Prophet and it was said to him, "Convert – if you convert, we will not kill you." So he converted and was not killed.*[102]

This offer to Furat was also reported by al-Tabari:

> *Furat b. Hayyan al-'Ijli was taken captive. They said to him, "If you accept Islam, the Messenger of God will not kill you." When the Messenger of God summoned him to Islam, he accepted it, and was allowed to go free.*[103]

In April 624 Muhammad had given the Jewish Banu Qaynuqa tribe the option of converting to Islam or fighting the Muslims. Now, about seven months later, he was more direct and in his presence an individual was given the stark choice of either converting to Islam or being killed.


## March 24, 625 – Muhammad Speaks for Allah

During this month the Muslims engaged in another major battle with the Meccans: The Battle of Uhud. The Muslims were defeated and they returned to Medina; the Meccans started heading back to Mecca. In what

---

[102]     *The Life of Muhammad: Al-Waqidi's Kitab al-Maghazi*, p. 99.

[103]     *The History of al-Tabari: The Foundation of the Community*, p. 99. It is interesting to note that in spite of what was reported in the three authoritative sources above, written within about 200 years after Muhammad's death, a 20th century award-winning biography of Muhammad claimed that Furat "embraced Islam out of his own free will"; see *The Sealed Nectar*, p. 291. Another modern biography, by the same author, described it this way: "The humane treatment Furat experienced at the hands of his captors so impressed him that he became Muslim"; see *When the Moon Split*, p. 211.

was an effort to show force, the Muslims left Medina in pursuit of the Meccans (this was known as the *Ghazwah* of Hamra' Al-Asad).

Prior to going in pursuit Muhammad had commanded a Muslim to call out, "The Messenger of God commands you to seek out your enemy…" On hearing this, one of the Muslim warriors, who had been wounded in the previous battle, called out, "Hear and obey God and His Prophet."[104] Many other wounded warriors responded to this call, and as a result, 3:172 was "revealed":[105]

> *Those who answered (the Call of) Allah and the Messenger (Muhammad) after being wounded; for those of them who did good deeds and feared Allah, there is a great reward.*

So here we have a Muslim warrior actually considering a command from Muhammad as being a command that came from Muhammad <u>and</u> Allah, and reporting it accordingly, with a subsequent "revelation" from Allah confirming this.

And it was around this time that another verse was "revealed" commanding Muslims to obey Allah and Muhammad:[106]

Chapter 3, Verse 132

> *And obey Allah and the Messenger (Muhammad) that you may obtain mercy.*

---

[104]  *The Life of Muhammad: Al-Waqidi's Kitab al-Maghazi*, p. 163.

[105]  *Tafsir Ibn Kathir*, Vol. 2, pp. 323-324; *Tafsir Ahsanul-Bayan*, Vol. 1, p. 392; *Tafsir as-Sa'di*, Vol. 1, p. 307; and *The Life of Muhammad: Al-Waqidi's Kitab al-Maghazi*, p. 165.

[106]  *The Meaning of the Glorious Koran*, p. 65.

## June 625 – June 626 – Obey Muhammad = Obey Allah

Chapter 4 of the Koran was, for the most part, "revealed" during this time period.[107] And in that chapter were numerous verses commanding Muslims to obey Allah and Muhammad (e.g. 4:13 and 4:69).

And there were even verses commanding the Muslims to specifically obey Muhammad, because it meant obeying Allah; and there were dire consequences for those who did not do so:

Chapter 4, Verse 65

> *But no, by your Lord, they can have no Faith, until they make you (O Muhammad) judge in all disputes between them, and find in themselves no resistance against your decisions, and accept (them) with full submission.*

Ibn Kathir explained this verse:

> *...no one shall attain faith until he refers to the Messenger for judgment in all matters. Thereafter, whatever the Messenger commands, is the plain truth that must be submitted to inwardly and outwardly.*[108]

And the following two verses were clear in their message:

Chapter 4, Verse 80

> *He who obeys the Messenger (Muhammad), has indeed obeyed Allah...*

---

[107]     Ibid., p. 91.

[108]     *Tafsir Ibn Kathir*, Vol. 2, p. 504.

50

Chapter 4, Verse 115

> *And whoever contradicts and opposes the Messenger*
> *(Muhammad) after the right path has been shown clearly*
> *to him, and follows other than the believers' way, We shall*
> *keep him in the path he has chosen, and burn him in Hell -*
> *what an evil destination!*

## **August 625 – No Compulsion, But Obey Muhammad**

At this time we have the "revelation" of the verse that prohibited forced conversions to Islam:

Chapter 2, Verse 256

> *There is no compulsion in religion. Verily, the Right Path*
> *has become distinct from the wrong path. Whoever*
> *disbelieves in Taghut and believes in Allah, then he has*
> *grasped the most trustworthy handhold that will never*
> *break. And Allah is All-Hearer, All-Knower.*

There are various reports about the cause for the "revelation" of 2:256. Al-Wahidi pointed out different narrators who explained the cause of this "revelation." These narrators referred to three different occurrences that led to the "revelation" of this verse:

1. Mujahid attributed it to a Muslim "who had a black boy" whom he used to try to coerce into becoming a Muslim;

2. Masruq and As-Suddi attributed it to a Muslim whose two sons converted to Christianity and Muhammad declined to do anything about it;[109]

---

[109]    As-Suddi commented on this occurrence:

3. Ibn 'Abbas and Mujahid attributed it to the Muslim expulsion of the Jewish Banu Nadir tribe in August 625. In this matter there were some children of Medinan Muslims being cared for by these Jews, and those children were leaving with the Jews to be raised as Jews; Muhammad refused to stop those children from leaving.[110]

Ibn Kathir also stated that ibn 'Abbas attributed the "revelation" of 2:256 to the Muslim expulsion of the Banu Nadir, and this same time frame was implied in the *Tafsir Al-Jalalayn*.[111]

Occurrences 2 and 3 were also mentioned by the Muslim scholar al-Qurtubi, who attributed the report about Occurrence No. 3 to ibn 'Abbas; al-Qurtubi quoted the Muslim scholar An-Nahhas who said that ibn 'Abbas' position on this was "the best position."[112]

And in *Sunan Abu Dawud*, there is an authoritative *hadith* in which ibn 'Abbas stated that 2:256 was "revealed" in reference to Occurrence 3.[113]

---

*This was before the Messenger of Allah, Allah bless him and give him peace, was commanded to fight the people of the Book. But then Allah's saying (There is no compulsion in religion...) was abrogated and the Prophet was commanded to fight the people of the Book in Surah Repentance [Koran Chapter 9].*

*Al-Wahidi's Asbab al-Nuzul*, p. 37. As-Suddi's statement about the abrogation of 2:256 was also reported in *Tafsir Al-Qurtubi*, p. 661. Allah's command to fight the People of the Book is found in 9:29.

[110]     *Al-Wahidi's Asbab al-Nuzul*, pp. 36-37.

[111]     *Tafsir Ibn Kathir*, Vol. 2, p. 30; and *Tafsir Al-Jalalayn*, p. 97.

[112]     *Tafsir Al-Qurtubi*, pp. 660-661.

[113]     *Sunan Abu Dawud*, Vol. 3, No. 2682, pp. 304-305.

Consequently, I will use the time frame of August 625 for the "revelation" of 2:256, with this "revelation" having occurred during the actual Muslim expulsion of the Banu Nadir.

However, there were other verses of the Koran "revealed" about the expulsion of the Banu Nadir. In fact, Chapter 59 of the Koran was "revealed" about the Muslim attack on, and the subsequent expulsion of the Banu Nadir tribe.[114]

And after the Jews were defeated and expelled from their lands, Muhammad assumed responsibility for the final disposition of their property. In relationship to the disposition of this property, 59:7 was "revealed." Here is part of that verse:

> *What Allah gave as booty to His Messenger*
> *(Muhammad)...And whatsoever the Messenger*
> *(Muhammad) gives you, take it; and whatsoever he*
> *forbids you, abstain (from it). And fear Allah; verily,*
> *Allah is Severe in punishment.*

Is this command from Allah to take whatever Muhammad gave, and abstain from whatever he forbade, general or just specific to the division of the property of the Banu Nadir? Here is what our *tafsirs* say about this verse.

The *Tafsir Ibn Kathir*, under the heading of *Ordering Obedience of the Messenger in All Commands and Prohibitions*:

---

[114]     *In Defence of the True Faith: Battles, Expeditions, Peace Treaties and their Consequences in the life of Prophet Muhammad*, p. 152; *The Life of Muhammad (Sirat Rasul Allah)*, p. 438; *The Life of Muhammad: Al-Waqidi's Kitab al-Maghazi*, pp. 186-188; *Tafsir Ibn Kathir*, Vol. 9, pp. 542 and 548; *Tafsir Ahsanul-Bayan*, Vol. 5, p. 397; *Sahih Muslim*, Vol. 8, No. 3031, p. 404; and Ma'mar ibn Rashid, *The Expeditions (Kitab al-Maghazi)*, trans. Sean W. Anthony (New York: New York University Press/Library of Arabic Literature, 2014), pp. 71-73.

*Allah the Exalted said, (And whatsoever the Messenger gives you, take it; and whatsoever he forbids you, abstain (from it.), meaning, 'whatever the Messenger commands you, then do it and whatever he forbids you, then avoid it. Surely, He only commands righteousness and forbids evil.*[115]

The *Tafsir Al-Jalalayn*:

**Whatever the Messenger gives you** by way of booty or anything else **you should accept; and whatever he forbids you, you should forgo.**[116]

The *Tafsir Ibn 'Abbas*:

*(And whatsoever the messenger giveth you) of spoils, (take it) accept it; it is also said that this means: whatever the messenger commands you, act upon it. (And whatsoever he forbideth, abstain (from it).*[117]

With regard to 59:7, the Muslim scholar Yasir Qadhi wrote:

*Is this verse then understood to apply only to the spoils of war, or does it apply to everything the Prophet commanded or forbade, since the wording of the verse implies this? The majority of scholars hold the view that the rulings from such verses are applied to every case that the wording of the verse covers.*[118]

---

[115]   *Tafsir Ibn Kathir*, Vol. 9, p. 558.

[116]   *Tafsir Al-Jalalayn*, p. 1187.

[117]   *Tafsir Ibn 'Abbas*, p. 755.

[118]   *An Introduction to the Sciences of the Qur'aan*, p. 117.

The Muslim scholar Sahl at-Tustari applied 59:7 to more than just the division of spoils. At-Tustari

> *was asked about the Shar'ia of Islam and he quoted, "Whatever the Messenger gives you you should accept." (59:7)*[119]

And to remove any uncertainty, Muhammad himself even weighed in on the matter as he equated his words with the Koran. He said:

> *Whoever clings to what I say and understands it and retains it, then it will be like the Qur'an for him. Whoever considers the Qur'an and what I say unimportant and neglects it loses this world and the Next. My community is commanded to take my words and obey my command and follow my sunna [sic]. Whoever is pleased with my words is pleased with the Qur'an. Allah says, 'Whatever the Messenger gives you you should accept.' (59:7)*[120]

This was repeated in the following *hadith* where, because of 59:7, whatever Muhammad permitted or forbade was also considered to have been permitted or forbidden in the Koran. In this *hadith*, a lady named Umm Ya'qub asked a Muslim named 'Abdullah why he had cursed some women for doing certain things. 'Abdullah replied:

> *"Why should I not curse these whom Allah's Messenger has cursed and who are (cursed) in Allah's Book!" Umm Ya'qub said, "I have read the whole Qur'an, but I did not find in it what you say." He said, "Verily, if you have read it (i.e., the Qur'an), you have found it. Didn't you*

---

[119]     Qadi 'Iyad ibn Musa al-Yahsubi, *Muhammad, Messenger of Allah: Ash-Shifa of Qadi 'Iyad*, trans. Aisha Abdarrahman Bewley (Norwich, UK: Diwan Press, 2011), p. 215. The *Shari'a* is the body of Islamic law - *Dictionary of Islamic Words & Expressions*, p. 215.

[120]     *Muhammad, Messenger of Allah: Ash-Shifa of Qadi 'Iyad*, p. 218.

*read: '...And whatsoever the Messenger (Muhammad) gives you take it and whatsoever he forbids you, you abstain (from it)...'" She replied "Yes, I did." He said, "Verily, Allah's Messenger forbade such things."*[121]

So we can see that 59:7 provided a Koranic basis for equating Muhammad's words with the commands of Allah in the Koran. And 59:7 was a general command to the Muslims to obey Muhammad in all his commands and prohibitions.

Prior to the "revelation" of 2:256 we had numerous examples of Koran verses, and statements and actions of Muhammad lending support to the idea of forced conversions to Islam. The "revelation" of 2:256 should have put an end to this. But, as we shall see, within a little over two years after that "revelation," the first of many such occurrences will take place in which Muhammad and his warriors gave non-Muslims the choice of converting to Islam or being killed (and at times including a third option of paying the *Jizyah*). Will Muhammad and his warriors be contradicting Allah and making permissible what Allah made impermissible?

The key to answering this question is the fact that 2:256 was "revealed" during the expulsion of the Banu Nadir tribe; but it was only after the tribe was expelled that all of their property could be gathered for distribution among the Muslims. Muhammad was the one who would decide how this property would be allocated, and 59:7 was then "revealed" to put Allah's approval on what Muhammad was doing; this verse ended with Allah's general command to take whatever Muhammad gave and abstain from whatever he forbade.

We can also see from Muhammad's statement and the above *hadith* that after 59:7 was "revealed," the Muslims understood that whatever Muhammad said, in effect the Koran said. And 59:7 was "revealed" after 2:256, so whenever there was a conflict between the messages of the two verses, the message of 2:256 would be abrogated by the message of 59:7.

---

[121]     *Sahih Al-Bukhari*, Vol. 6, Book 65, No. 4886, pp. 340-341.

# October 625 – Accepting New Geo-Political Conditions

During this time Muhammad led the Expedition of Dhat al-Riqa against the Bedouins of Najd. Muhammad was at the head of 400-700 Muslim warriors. The Muslims met an opposing force, but no actual fighting was reported.[122] However, there were reports that the Muslims had captured an unspecified number of non-Muslim women,[123] and that one of the Muslims had even killed a non-Muslim woman.[124]

---

[122]     There is some disagreement about when this expedition occurred. The approximate date of October 625 was used in *The Life of Muhammad (Sirat Rasul Allah)*, p. 445; this date was also mentioned in *The History of al-Tabari: The Foundation of the Community*, p. 161; and *In Defence of the True Faith: Battles, Expeditions, Peace Treaties and their Consequences in the life of Prophet Muhammad*, p. 163.

Ibn Sa'd reported that this expedition occurred around June 625; see *Kitab al-Tabaqat al-Kabir*, Vol. 2, p. 74.

Al-Waqidi stated that this expedition took place around July of 626 - see *The History of al-Tabari: The Foundation of the Community*, p. 161. The expedition was also reported to have occurred after the Battle of the Trench, which occurred in February 627; see *In Defence of the True Faith: Battles, Expeditions, Peace Treaties and their Consequences in the life of Prophet Muhammad*, p. 164.

But some claimed that this expedition actually occurred sometime after the Muslim conquest of Khaybar, which occurred around May 628 - see *Sahih Al-Bukhari*, Vol. 5, Book 64, Chapter 32, p. 273; *The Sealed Nectar*, p. 446; and *In Defence of the True Faith: Battles, Expeditions, Peace Treaties and their Consequences in the life of Prophet Muhammad*, pp. 163-164.

I have chosen to use the time frame mentioned in Ibn Ishaq's biography of Muhammad because Ibn Ishaq's estimate was noted by both al-Tabari and ibn Kathir.

[123]     *Kitab al-Tabaqat al-Kabir*, Vol. 2, p. 74; and *The Life of Muhammad: Al-Waqidi's Kitab al-Maghazi*, p. 194.

[124]     *The History of al-Tabari: The Foundation of the Community*, p. 164; *Sunan Abu Dawud*, Vol. 1, No. 198, pp. 130-131; *In Defence of the True Faith:*

57

A 20th Century biography of Muhammad pointed out that this expedition changed the relationship between the Muslims and the Bedouins:

> *The victory at the Invasion of Dhat-ur-Riqa' had a*
> *tremendous impact on all the bedouins* [sic]. *It cast fear*
> *into their hearts and made them too powerless to annoy*
> *the Muslim society in Madinah. They began to adjust in*
> *the prevailing situation and prepared themselves to accept*
> *the new geo-political conditions working in favor of the*
> *new religion. Some of them even embraced Islam and*
> *took an active part in the conquest of Makkah and the*
> *battle of Hunain, and received their due shares of the war*
> *booty.*[125]

As we can see, this changing relationship between the Bedouins and the Muslims came about not as a result of preaching about Islam, but rather as a result of the invasion of a large Muslim army that created a new "geo-political" condition. Relying on a Muslim religious doctrine of "no compulsion" seemed to have little appeal for the non-Muslims facing an invading force of 400-700 Muslim warriors.


## January 626 – Allah and Muhammad Have Decided

Here we have a Koran verse telling Muslims that they were prohibited from disagreeing with a command or decision from Allah and Muhammad. This verse was "revealed" because Muhammad wanted Zaynab bint Jahsh, a woman of some nobility, to marry Zayd bin Harithah. Zayd had originally been given to Muhammad as a slave; Muhammad subsequently freed Zayd and adopted him as his son. Because of Zayd's former status,

---

*Battles, Expeditions, Peace Treaties and their Consequences in the life of Prophet Muhammad*, p. 165; and *The Life of Muhammad (Sirat Rasul Allah)*, p. 447.

[125]     *The Sealed Nectar*, p. 446.

Zaynab was reluctant to engage in such a marriage until 33:36 was "revealed", and the marriage took place.[126] Here is that verse:

> *It is not for a believer, man or woman, when Allah and His Messenger, have decreed a matter that they should have any option in their decision. And whoever disobeys Allah and His Messenger, he has indeed strayed into a plain error.*

Ibn Kathir explained this verse quite simply:

> *This Ayah is general in meaning and applies to all matters, i.e., if Allah and His Messenger decreed a matter, no one has the right to go against that, and no one has any choice or room for personal opinion in this case.*[127]

The *Tafsir Al-Jalalayn* noted:

> **When Allah and His Messenger have decided something, it is not for any man or woman of the believers to have a**

---

[126]   *Tafsir Ahsanul-Bayan*, Vol. 4, pp. 388-389; *Tafsir Al-Jalalayn*, pp. 902-904; *Tafsir Ibn 'Abbas*, p. 548; *Men and Women Around the Messenger*, pp. 543-544; and *The Honourable Wives of the Prophet*, ed. Abdul Ahad (Riyadh, Kingdom of Saudi Arabia: Darussalam, 2004), pp. 122-123.

I determined the date of "revelation" as January 626 in this manner: Zayd and Zaynab were later divorced, and Muhammad married Zaynab in April 627 (*The Sealed Nectar*, p. 563; and Abu Ja'far Muhammad b. Jarir al-Tabari, *The History of al-Tabari: The Last Years of the Prophet*, Vol. IX, trans. and annotated Ismail K. Poonawala (Albany, New York: State University of New York Press, 1990), n. 895, p. 134). The waiting period (*'Iddah*) for Zaynab between her divorce and being able to marry again was about three months (Koran 2:228). The marriage of Zayd and Zaynab lasted about one year (*Tafsir Ibn Kathir*, Vol. 7, p. 696). Consequently, I put the date of the "revelation" of 33:36 to be around January 626.

[127]   *Tafsir Ibn Kathir*, Vol. 7, p. 694.

***choice about it*** *– to want something different from what*
*Allah and His Messenger have commanded.*[128]

The *Tafsir Ahsanul-Bayan* explained that this verse

> *said in no unclear terms that it was not permissible for*
> *believers to have a say in a matter already decided by*
> *Allah and His Messenger. Their duty is just to submit to*
> *Allah's will and His Prophet's, without demur.*[129]

## June 625 - May 627 - Follow Muhammad's Example

During this time period Koran Chapter 58 was "revealed,"[130] and there
were two verses in particular that emphasized that Muslims were to obey
Allah and Muhammad, and opposition to this would be punished:

Chapter 58, Verse 5

> *Verily, those who oppose Allah and His Messenger*
> *(Muhammad), will be disgraced as those before them*
> *(among the past nations) were disgraced...*

Chapter 58, Verse 20

> *Those who oppose Allah and His Messenger*
> *(Muhammad), they will be among the lowest (most*
> *humiliated).*

---

128    *Tafsir Al-Jalalayn*, p. 902.

129    *Tafsir Ahsanul-Bayan*, Vol. 4, p. 389.

130    *The Meaning of the Glorious Koran*, p. 570.

After the Battle of the Trench (also known as the Battle of the Confederates) in February 627, a verse of the Koran was "revealed" stating that Muhammad was the timeless standard by which Muslims should conduct themselves:

Chapter 33, Verse 21

> *Indeed in the Messenger of Allah (Muhammad) you have a good example to follow for him who hopes for (the Meeting with) Allah and the Last Day, and remembers Allah much.*

In a section titled *The Command to follow the Messenger*, Ibn Kathir wrote about this verse:

> *This Ayah is an important principle, to follow the Messenger of Allah in all his words, and deeds...* [131]

The *Tafsir Al-Jalalayn* explained:

> **You have an excellent model in the Messenger of Allah –** *with regard to imitating him in fighting and in remaining firm in his position...* [132]

And the *Tafsir Ahsanul-Bayan* noted that this verse had a general meaning:

> *Although the Verse was revealed in the context of the Battle of Confederates* [sic]*...the commandment is general. That is, he is a paragon worth emulating in all matters...* [133]

---

[131]    *Tafsir Ibn Kathir*, Vol. 7, p. 658.

[132]    *Tafsir Al-Jalalayn*, p. 900.

[133]    *Tafsir Ahsanul-Bayan*, Vol. 4, p. 374.

# 6

# Convert to Islam or Else (627–630)

In August 625 the verse forbidding forced conversions to Islam had been "revealed." In theory, there were to be no more forced conversions. But within a little over two years that was to change.

## December 627 – An "Invitation" to Dumat al-Jandal

In December 627 Muhammad sent a Muslim force of 700 men under the command of 'Abd al-Rahman bin 'Awf to Dumat al-Jandal to "invite them to Islam." Muhammad commanded 'Abd al-Rahman:

> *Take it* [the standard], *Ibn 'Auf; fight everyone in the way of God and kill those who disbelieve in God...This is God's ordinance and the practice of his prophet among you.*[134]

---

[134]   *The Life of Muhammad (Sirat Rasul Allah)*, p. 672. There were some slight variations in how Muhammad's command was reported, but the message of Muhammad's command was to fight anyone who was a non-Muslim:

> *In the name of Allah and in the way of Allah fight him who believes not in Allah.*

*Kitab al-Tabaqat al-Kabir*, Vol. 2, p. 110.

> *Attack in the name of God, and in the way of God and fight those who disbelieve in God.*

*The Life of Muhammad: Al-Waqidi's Kitab al-Maghazi*, p. 275.

When the Muslim force arrived, 'Abd al-Rahman

> *invited the people to Islam, and stayed there for three days*
> *inviting them to Islam. At first they refused all but the*
> *sword.*[135]

On the third day of battle their Christian leader converted to Islam, and the people of Dumat al-Jandal soon converted too.

## March 628 – Make Islam Victorious Over All Religions

During this time Muhammad, accompanied by about 1,400 Muslims, travelled to Mecca to perform the "lesser pilgrimage" (*'Umrah*) and visit the Ka'bah. The Quraysh in Mecca did not want him to enter Mecca and sent out a military force. Muhammad evaded the force and camped at al-Hudaybiyah, making no effort to enter Mecca. This resulted in a treaty between Muhammad and the Quraysh that, among other things, guaranteed ten years of peace between them and would allow Muhammad to make the pilgrimage to Mecca the following year. This was known as the Treaty of Al-Hudaybiyah, and it lasted less than two years.

Chapter 61 of the Koran may have been "revealed" while the Muslims were camped at al-Hudaybiyah.[136] This chapter has an interesting verse that proclaims that Islam will be victorious over all other religions, even if the non-Muslims don't like it:

Chapter 61, Verse 9

> *He it is Who has sent his Messenger (Muhammad) with*
> *guidance and the religion of truth (Islamic Monotheism)*
> *to make it victorious over all (other) religions even though*

---

[135]    *The Life of Muhammad: Al-Waqidi's Kitab al-Maghazi*, pp. 275-276.

[136]    *The Meaning of the Glorious Koran*, p. 582.

*the Mushrikun (polytheists, pagans, idolaters, and
disbelievers in the Oneness of Allah and in His Messenger
Muhammad) hate (it).*

And while camped at al-Hudaybiyah, Muhammad emphasized the
importance of following his "practices" and the commands of Allah:

> *He spoke to the people and said, "O People, indeed I exist
> for you as a reward. I leave with you, in your hands, what
> will not lead you astray, the book of God and its
> practices." And some say that he said, "I have left with
> you the Book of God and the practices of His Prophet."* [137]

While encamped, Muhammad also told the Muslims that they had not
come with the intent to fight the Quraysh, because the Quraysh had been
weakened by war. Muhammad said that what he wanted was a treaty with
the Quraysh that would allow the Muslims to fight the "Arab infidels" and,
by force, convince those infidels to become Muslims. He said that after
the victory over the "Arab infidels," the Quraysh would then have the
option to also "embrace Islam." If the Quraysh refused the treaty, or
refused to embrace Islam after the other "Arab infidels" had done so, then
the Muslims would fight the Quraysh until Islam was victorious or
Muhammad was killed.

There are multiple reports from our authoritative sources about this
statement by Muhammad:

*Abridged Biography of Prophet Muhammad*

> *We have not come to fight; we have only come to perform
> 'Umrah and Quraish have been weakened and harmed by
> war and if they wish I will conclude a truce with them,
> during which they should refrain from interfering between
> me and the people (i.e. the Arab infidels other than*

---

[137]  *The Life of Muhammad: Al-Waqidi's Kitab al-Maghazi*, p. 284.

*Quraish), and if I have victory over those infidels, Quraish will have the option to embrace Islam as the other people do, if they wish; they will at least get strong enough to fight. But if they do not accept the truce, by Allah in Whose Hands my life is, I will fight with them defending my Cause till I get killed, but (I am sure) Allah will definitely make His Cause victorious.[138]*

## *The Expeditions (Kitab al-Maghazi)*

*We have not come to battle against anyone. Rather, we have come as pilgrims. War has exhausted the Quraysh and brought them to ruin. If they wish, I shall grant them a period of respite, but they must leave me and the people alone. If I prevail, and if they wish to join the people in embracing Islam, then they may do so. If not, and if, after having gathered their strength, they refuse, then by Him in Whose hand my soul resides, I will not hesitate to fight against them for the sake of this cause of mine until my neck is severed! Surely God will see His cause through to the end.[139]*

## *The History of al-Tabari: The Victory of Islam*

*We have not come to fight anyone; we have come to make the lesser pilgrimage. War has exhausted and harmed Quraysh. If they wish, we will grant them a delay, and*

---

[138]    *Abridged Biography of Prophet Muhammad*, p. 232; this was also reported in *Sahih Al-Bukhari*, Vol. 3, Book 54, Nos. 2731-2732, p. 529. This statement by Muhammed was reported, with virtually the same wording, in *In Defence of the True Faith: Battles, Expeditions, Peace Treaties and their Consequences in the life of Prophet Muhammad*, p. 255.

[139]    *The Expeditions (Kitab al-Maghazi)*, p. 29.

*they can leave me to deal with the people* [the Arabs]. *If I am victorious, if they wish to enter that which the people enter* [Islam] *they can do so; if not, they will have rested and recovered their strength. If they refuse [the delay], by Him who holds my soul in His hand, I shall fight them for the sake of this affair of mine until the side of my neck becomes separated or God effects his command.*[140]

## The Life of Muhammad (Sirat Rasul Allah)

*Alas, Quraysh, war has devoured them! What harm would they have suffered if they had left me and the rest of the Arabs to go our own ways? If they should kill me that is what they desire, and if God should give me the victory over them they would enter Islam in flocks. If they do not do that they will fight while they have the strength, so what are Quraysh thinking of? By Allah, I will not cease to fight for the mission with which God has entrusted me until He makes it victorious or I perish.*[141]

After the Treaty of Al-Hudaybiyah was signed, Chapter 48 of the Koran was "revealed."[142] In this chapter we have verses commanding the Muslims to obey Allah and Muhammad (48:13 and 48:17), and a verse stating that Muhammad would triumph and Islam would be made superior to all other religions:

---

[140]    Abu Ja'far Muhammad b. Jarir al-Tabari, *The History of al-Tabari: The Victory of Islam*, Vol. VIII, trans. and annotated Michael Fishbein (Albany, New York: State University of New York Press, 1997), p. 75.

[141]    *The Life of Muhammad (Sirat Rasul Allah)*, p. 500.

[142]    *Al-Wahidi's Asbab al-Nuzul*, p. 201; *Tafsir Ibn Kathir*, Vol. 9, p. 122; *Tafsir Ahsanul-Bayan*, Vol. 5, pp. 174-175; *Tafsir Al-Jalalayn*, p. 1097; *The Life of Muhammad (Sirat Rasul Allah)*, p. 505; and *The Meaning of the Glorious Koran*, pp. 527-528.

Chapter 48, Verse 28

> *He it is Who has sent His Messenger (Muhammad) with*
> *guidance and the religion of truth (Islam), that He may*
> *make it (Islam) superior to all religions.  And All-*
> *Sufficient is Allah as a Witness.*

And in 48:29 we have a verse admonishing the Muslims to be "severe"
against the non-Muslims and "merciful" among themselves:

> *Muhammad is the Messenger of Allah.  And those who are*
> *with him are severe against disbelievers, and merciful*
> *among themselves...*

## March 628 – Verse 48:16 Abrogates 2:256

Of greatest significance for us among the verses in Chapter 48 is:

Chapter 48, Verse 16

> *Say (O Muhammad) to the bedouins who lagged behind:*
> *"You shall be called to fight against a people given to*
> *great warfare, then you shall fight them, or they shall*
> *surrender..."*

The *Tafsir Ahsanul-Bayan* explained this verse:

> *...the Bedouin who were left behind were told to be ready*
> *to fight a warlike people in case the latter did not become*
> *Muslims.*[143]

So "a warlike people" were to be given the choice of converting to Islam
or fighting.  According to Ibn Kathir, 48:16 abrogated 2:256.[144]

---

[143]     *Tafsir Ahsanul-Bayan*, Vol. 5, p. 185.

## April - May 628 – A Grace Period for Non-Muslims

In this incident Muhammad "invited" a tribe to Islam, and gave a grace period of only two months to those who did not become Muslims:

> *Rifa'a b. Zayd al-Judhami of the clan of al-Dubayb came to the apostle during the armistice of al-Hudaybiya before Khaybar. He gave the apostle a slave and he became a good Muslim. The apostle gave him a letter to his people in which he wrote: To Rifa'a b. Zayd whom I have sent to his people and those who have joined them to invite them to God and His apostle. Whosoever comes forward is of the party of God and His apostle, and whosoever turns back has two months' grace.[145]*

Rifa'a's people accepted Islam.


## June 628 – "Invitations" to Khaybar and Fadak

Muhammad now turned his sights on the Jewish community of Khaybar and led a Muslim army of 1,400 toward that community. Once the Muslims were ready to attack, Muhammad put his cousin Ali in charge of the army. When Ali asked on what basis they were to fight this Jewish

---

[144]      Abu al-Fida' 'Imad Ad-Din Isma'il bin 'Umar bin Kathir al-Qurashi Al-Busrawi, *Tafsir Ibn Kathir* (Abridged), abr. Sheikh Muhammad Nasib Ar-Rafa'i, trans. Chafik Abdelghani ibn Rahal (London: Al-Firdous Ltd., 1998), Part 3, p. 38.

[145]      *The Life of Muhammad (Sirat Rasul Allah)*, p. 648; this incident, with the two month grace period for those refusing Islam, was also mentioned in *Kitab al-Tabaqat al-Kabir*, Vol. 1, p. 416; and *The Life of Muhammad: Al-Waqidi's Kitab al-Maghazi*, p. 273. Al-Waqidi provided a different time frame for this incident, writing that it occurred at the time of Zayd B. Haritha's expedition to Hisma, which was around October 627.

community, Muhammad replied that they were to be fought until they accepted Islam:

> *Suhail reported on the authority of Abu Huraira that Allah's Messenger (may peace be upon him) said on the Day of Khaibar: I shall certainly give this standard in the hand of one who loves Allah and His Messenger and Allah will grant victory at his hand...Allah's Messenger (may peace be upon him) called Ali b. Abu Talib and he conferred (this honour) upon him and said: Proceed on and do not look about until Allah grants you victory, and Ali went a bit and then halted and did not look about and then said in a loud voice: Allah's Messenger, on what issue should I fight with the people? There upon he (the Prophet) said: Fight with them until they testify that there is no god but Allah and Muhammad is His Messenger, and when they do that, then their blood and their riches are inviolable from your hands. But what is justified by law and their reckoning is with Allah.*[146]

Muhammad's command to fight the Jews of Khaybar until they accepted Islam was reported in other sources:

*Kitab al-Tabaqat al-Kabir*

> [*'Ali*] *went close (to the ranks of enemy) and cried: O Apostle of Allah! for* [sic] *what should I fight? He replied: (Fight) until they bear witness (to the truth) that there is no god save Allah and that Muhammad is the Apostle of Allah. When they confess this, their persons and properties will be saved from me except in the discharge of their obligations and their reckoning will be with Allah.*[147]

---

[146]     *Sahih Muslim*, Vol. 7, No. 2405, p. 85.

[147]     *Kitab al-Tabaqat al-Kabir*, Vol. 2, p. 137.

> *The Prophet instructed him* ['Ali] *to invite the enemy to Islam. Only if they rejected the call to faith was Ali to fight.*[148]

The Muslims attacked Khaybar at daybreak, as the townspeople were coming out of their houses to go to their jobs. Khaybar was conquered, and the "women of Khaybar were distributed among the Muslims."[149] The war-cry of the Muslims had been, "O victorious one, slay, slay!"[150]

On the way to Khaybar, the Muslims had captured a Bedouin spy sent by the Jews. The spy had been tied up and kept with a Muslim warrior. After the Muslims entered Khaybar, Muhammad offered the spy the option of converting to Islam or being hung:

> *When the Messenger of God entered Khaybar, he proposed Islam to him. The Messenger of God said, "Indeed I invite you," three times. "If you do not convert, he will not take off the rope from your neck except to go up – hang." The Bedouin converted.*[151]

## Fadak

In the area of Khaybar was the town of Fadak. Muhammad

> *sent Muhayyisa b. Mas'ud to invite the people of Fadak to Islam, filling them with fear that they would attack them*

---

148     *When the Moon Split*, p. 299.

149     *The Life of Muhammad (Sirat Rasul Allah)*, p. 511.

150     Ibid., n. 760, p. 770.

151     *The Life of Muhammad: Al-Waqidi's Kitab al-Maghazi*, p. 316.

*as they had attacked the people of Khaybar, and descend on their fields.*[152]

A modern biography of Muhammad added:

*Once the Prophet arrived at Khaybar, he sent Mahisa bin Mas'ood eastward to the township of Fadak...The Jews there were also called on to accept Islam, but they held off their reply, waiting to see which way the battel for Khaybar went. The conquest of Khaybar propelled them into starting negotiations...*[153]

As Ibn Ishaq explained it:

*When the apostle had finished with Khaybar, God struck terror to the hearts of the men of Fadak when they heard what the apostle had done to the men of Khaybar. They sent to him an offer of peace on condition that they should keep half of their produce...and he accepted their terms. Thus Fadak became his private property, because it had not been attacked by horse or camel.*[154]

Al-Baladhuri provided a similar explanation in a section titled *The capitulation* [sic] *of Fadak*:

*As the Prophet departed from Khaibar, he sent to the people of Fadak Muhaiyisah ibn-Mas'ud al-Ansari inviting them to Islam...They made terms with the Prophet, agreeing to give up one-half of the land with its soil. The Prophet accepted. Thus one-half was assigned*

---

[152]   Ibid., p. 347.

[153]   *When the Moon Split*, p. 303.

[154]   *The Life of Muhammad (Sirat Rasul Allah)*, p. 523.

71

*wholly to the Prophet because the Moslems "pressed not*
*against it with horse or camel."[155]*

## June 628 – An "Invitation" to Wadi al-Qura

On the way back to Medina from Khaybar, Muhammad stopped in the
Jewish town of Wadi al-Qura:

> *The Messenger of God charged his companions to*
> *fight…Then the Messenger of God invited the Jews to*
> *Islam. He informed them that if they converted they would*
> *keep their property and retain their blood…[156]*

But the Jews decided to fight:

> *They fought each other until evening…when they*
> *surrendered. He [Muhammad] conquered them by force.*
> *God plundered their property and they took furniture and*
> *goods in plenty.[157]*

There was another report that Muhammad had offered the Jews their
property and lives if they converted to Islam:

> *The Messenger of Allah, peace and blessings of Allah be*
> *upon him, prevented his Companions from fighting*
> *against them. Rather, he arrayed them and then invited*

---

[155]     Ahmad ibn Yahya ibn Jabir al-Baladhuri, *The Origins of the Islamic*
*State, Being a Translation from the Arabic, Accompanied with Annotations,*
*Geographic and Historic Notes of the Kitab Fituh Al-Buldan of Al-Imam Abu-L*
*Abbas Ahmad Ibn-Jabir Al-Baladhuri*, trans. Philip Khuri Hitti (1916; rpt.
Lexington, Kentucky: Ulan Press, 2014), p. 50.

[156]     *The Life of Muhammad: Al-Waqidi's Kitab al-Maghazi*, p. 349.

[157]     Ibid., p. 350.

*them to Islam and informed them that if they accept Islam,*
*they will be protecting their wealth and preserving their*
*blood, and their accounting rests with Allah, the*
*Almighty.*[158]

And there were other reports that Muhammad had simply invited the Jews
to Islam before the fighting started:

*When the Prophet departed from Khaibar, he went to*
*Wadi-l-Kura and invited its people to Islam. They refused*
*and started hostilities. The Prophet reduced the place by*
*force; and Allah gave him as booty the possessions of its*
*inhabitants.*[159]

**And:**

*No sooner than the Prophet had discharged the affair of*
*Khaibar, he started a fresh move towards Wadi Al-Qura,*
*another Jewish colony in Arabia...Prior to fighting, he*
*invited the Jews to embrace Islam but all his words fell on*
*deaf ears. Eleven of the Jews were killed one after*
*another and with each one newly killed, a fresh call was*
*extended inviting those people to profess the new faith.*
*Fighting went on ceaselessly for approximately two days*
*and resulted in full surrender of the Jews. Their land was*
*conquered, and a lot of booty fell in the hands of the*
*Muslims.*[160]

---

[158]    *In Defence of the True Faith: Battles, Expeditions, Peace Treaties and*
*their Consequences in the life of Prophet Muhammad*, p. 294.

[159]    *The Origins of the Islamic State*, p. 57. That the Jews rejected
Muhammad's "invitation" to Islam and were subsequently defeated in battle was
also mentioned in *Abridged Biography of Prophet Muhammad*, pp. 244-245.

[160]    *The Sealed Nectar*, p. 442. A similar narrative about repeated invitations
to Islam is found in *When the Moon Split*, p. 304.

## March 629 – Fight Them Until They Accept Islam

During this time a verse of the Koran was "revealed" that commanded Muslims to fight non-Muslims until they accepted Islam.[161] Whether they were hostile toward the Muslims or not was irrelevant; the mere fact that they were non-Muslims was enough to allow the Muslims to initiate the fighting:

Chapter 2, Verse 193

> *And fight them until there is no more Fitnah (disbelief and worshipping of others along with Allah) and (all and every kind of ) worship is for Allah (Alone). But if they cease, let there be no transgression except against Az-Zalimun (the polytheists and wrongdoers).*

The authoritative Muslim scholar al-Qurtubi explained this verse:

> *It is an unqualified command to fight without any precondition of hostilities being initiated by the unbelievers. The evidence for that is in the words of Allah, "and the din* [religion] *belongs to Allah alone."*

---

[161]     There were two reports that this verse was among those "revealed" around the time of Muhammad's "Fulfilled Pilgrimage" to Mecca in March 629; see *Al-Wahidi's Asbab al-Nuzul*, p. 23; and *Tafsir Ahsanul-Bayan*, Vol. 1, pp. 171-172. In addition, al-Qurtubi wrote that 2:190 was "revealed" concerning the "Fulfilled Pilgrimage" and agreed with those who said 2:193 had subsequently abrogated those "previous" verses – see *Tafsir Al-Qurtubi*, pp. 490 and 496. Consequently, I am using the date of March 629 for the "revelation" of this verse.

There were two other dates mentioned for the "revelation" of 2:193. Ibn Ishaq wrote that this verse was "revealed" just prior to the Muslim emigration to Medina in July 622 – see *The Life of Muhammad (Sirat Rasul Allah)*, p. 213 (this verse was erroneously listed as "2:198" in the corresponding footnote). However, in a 20th Century biography of Muhammad it was reported that this verse was "revealed" in February 624 - *The Sealed Nectar*, pp. 247-248.

*The Prophet said, "I was commanded to fight people until they say, 'There is no god but Allah.' The ayat [verse] and hadith both indicate that the reason for fighting is disbelief...**If they cease, there should be no enmity towards any but wrongdoers.** If they stop and become Muslim or submit by paying jizya in the case of the people of the Book. Otherwise they should be fought and they are wrongdoers....The wrongdoers are either those who initiate fighting or those who remain entrenched in disbelief and fitna.*[162]

Ibn Kathir explained this verse in a section titled *The Order to fight until there is no more Fitnah*:

*Allah then commanded fighting the disbelievers when He said: "...until there is no more Fitnah" meaning, Shirk...Allah's statement: "...and the religion (all and every kind of worship) is for Allah (Alone)" means, 'So that the religion of Allah becomes dominant above all other religions.*'[163]

Ibn Kathir went on to explain *But if they cease* indicated:

*If they stop their Shirk and fighting the believers, then cease warfare against them.*[164]

The *Tafsir Al-Jalalayn* explained that this verse meant to fight "until there is no more fitna (*shirk*) in existence" and none but Allah is worshipped.[165]

---

[162]   *Tafsir Al-Qurtubi*, p. 496.

[163]   *Tafsir Ibn Kathir*, Vol. 1, p. 531.

[164]   Ibid., p. 532.

[165]   *Tafsir Al-Jalalayn*, p. 69.

75

And the *Tafsir As-Sa'di* pointed out:

> ...*Allah explains the goals of participating in fighting and jihad in His cause. Fighting in Allah's cause is not just for shedding the blood of the disbelievers and taking their possessions [as spoils]; rather, its sole goal is that* **worship is [solely] for Allah**, *to achieve superiority of Allah's religion over all other religions and faiths, and to eradicate idolatry, atheism, and other such theologies from this earth for good.*[166]

There is an irreconcilable contradiction between the message of 2:256 and that of 2:193. Based on the timing of the respective "revelations," it appears that 2:193 joined 48:16 in abrogating 2:256 and consequently provided additional support for Muhammad's subsequent actions.

## April 629 – An "Invitation" to the Banu Sulaym

After he returned from his "Fulfilled Pilgrimage" Muhammad sent a force of 51 Muslim fighters to the Banu Sulaym to "invite" them to Islam. The Banu Sulaym refused and a battle ensued. The Muslims were defeated and there were varying reports about the number of their casualties.[167] The Banu Sulaym did not convert to Islam at this time.

## May 629 – Muhammad's Letter to Hajar

In this month Muhammad sent a letter to the leader of the people of Hajar "inviting" them to become Muslims or to pay the *Jizyah*. When the leader showed Muhammad's letter to his people, they all agreed to pay the *Jizyah*

---

[166]    *Tafsir As-Sa'di*, Vol. 1, p. 134.

[167]    *The Life of Muhammad: Al-Waqidi's Kitab al-Maghazi*, p. 365; *Kitab al-Tabaqat al-Kabir*, Vol. 2, p. 153; *The Sealed Nectar*, p. 451; *The History of al-Tabari: The Victory of Islam*, p. 138.

because they disliked the idea of becoming Muslims. However, Muhammad accepted that decision only from the non-Arabs; he said the Arabs had a choice of either Islam or the sword:

> *Al-Kalbi reported from Abu Salih who related that Ibn 'Abbas said: "The Messenger of Allah sent a letter to the people of Hajar, whose chief was Mundhir ibn Sawa, inviting them to Islam, or to pay the Jizyah if they chose not to embrace Islam. When Mundhir ibn Sawa received the letter, he showed it to the Arabs, Jews, Christians, Sabeans and Magians who were around him. They all agreed to pay the Jizyah and disliked embracing Islam. The Messenger of Allah, Allah bless him and give him peace, wrote back to him, saying: As for the Arabs, do not accept from them except Islam [sic] otherwise they will have nothing but the sword. As for the people of the Book and the Magians, accept the Jizyah from them. When this letter was read to them, the Arabs embraced Islam while the people of the Book and the Magians agreed to pay the Jizyah..."[168]*

It was reported that Muhammad ended up writing a separate letter to the Magians:

> *The Apostle of Allah, may Allah bless him, wrote an epistle to the Magians of Hajar presenting Islam to them. In case they declined the offer, they would have to pay jizyah and their women would not be married (to Muslims) and the meat of animals slaughtered by them would not be eaten (by Muslims).[169]*

---

[168]    *Al-Wahidi's Asbab al-Nuzul*, p. 102. For further details of this matter, see *The Origins of the Islamic State*, pp. 120-124.

[169]    *Kitab al-Tabaqat al-Kabir*, Vol. 1, pp. 310-311. For a similar report about Muhammad's letter to the Magians, see *The Origins of the Islamic State*, p. 123. Here is an interesting *hadith* about the results of a Magian meeting with Muhammad at some unspecified time:

## July 629 – An "Invitation" to Dhat Atlah

Muhammad sent 15 men under the command of Ka'b b. 'Umayr al-Ghifari to Dhat Atlah. The expedition came across "one of the larger groups and invited them to Islam." A battle ensued and all of the Muslims but one was killed.[170] There were no reported conversions to Islam.

## August-September 629 – Three Options for Mu'ta

Muhammad sent a force of 3,000 Muslims under the command of Zayd bin Harithah to Mu'ta. Muhammad commanded Zayd to give the enemy the choice between converting to Islam, paying the *Jizyah*, or fighting:

> *Raid, in the name of God and in the path of God, and fight those who disbelieve in God...If you meet your enemy from the polytheists, ask them one of three questions...Invite them to enter Islam. If they do, accept them and refrain from them...If they refuse, invite them to pay the jizya, and if they agree to pay the jizya, accept them and refrain from them. If they refuse, ask God's help and fight them.[171]*

---

*Sulaiman bin Moosa narrated that 'Abdur-Rahman bin 'Awf said: When the Majoosi [Magian] came out from the presence of the Messenger of Allah I asked him, and he told me that the Prophet had given him the choice between paying the jizyah or execution, and he chose to pay the jizyah.*

*Musnad Imam Ahmad Bin Hanbal*, Vol. 2, No. 1672, pp. 135-136.

---

[170]    *The Life of Muhammad: Al-Waqidi's Kitab al-Maghazi*, p. 370. Also see *Kitab al-Tabaqat al-Kabir*, Vol. 2, p. 158; *In Defence of the True Faith: Battles, Expeditions, Peace Treaties and their Consequences in the life of Prophet Muhammad*, pp. 313-314; *The Sealed Nectar*, p. 451; and *The History of al-Tabari: The Victory of Islam*, p. 143.

[171]    *The Life of Muhammad: Al-Waqidi's Kitab al-Maghazi*, pp. 372-373.

However, there were other reports that Muhammad commanded Zayd to give the enemy the simple choice of either converting to Islam or fighting:

*The Sealed Nectar*

> *The Prophet recommended that they reach the scene of Al-Harith's murder and invite the people to profess Islam. Should the latter respond positively, then no war would follow, otherwise fighting them would be the only alternative. He ordered them: Fight the disbelievers in the Name of Allah...*[172]

*Kitab al-Tabaqat al-Kabir*

> *The Apostle of Allah, may Allah bless him, advised him [Zayd] to reach the site of the slaying of al-Harith Ibn 'Umayr, and invite them to join the fold of Islam, if they respond, it is good, otherwise seek Divine succour [sic] and fight them.*[173]

*When the Moon Split*

> *The Prophet prepared a white standard and handed it to Zayd bin Haritha. He instructed Zayd to go to the area where Harith had been martyred, and to invite the populace to Islam. The Muslims were to fight only if the people rejected the call.*[174]

---

[172]    *The Sealed Nectar*, pp. 452-453.

[173]    *Kitab al-Tabaqat al-Kabir*, Vol. 2, p. 159.

[174]    *When the Moon Split*, p. 311.

The Muslims did not anticipate the overwhelming size of the enemy forces arrayed against them. The Muslims were defeated and returned to Medina.


## January 630 – Meccans Accept Islam, Willingly or Not

In this month Muhammad led a force of 10,000 Muslim warriors against Mecca. Prior to the attack the Muslim army was encamped outside of Mecca at Marr al-Zahran. Muhammad's uncle, al-'Abbas, realized that the non-Muslim Quraysh tribe of Mecca was facing potential devastation:

> *When the Messenger of God encamped at Marr al-Zahran, al-'Abbas b. 'Abd al-Muttalib said...Woe to Quraysh! If the Messenger of God surprises them in their territory and enters Mecca by force, it means the destruction of Quraysh forever.[175]*

There was a report that al-'Abbas was so concerned about the people of Mecca that he actually went to Mecca to warn them that only by converting to Islam would they be safe:

> *Al-'Abbas asked the Prophet saying, "Send me to the people of Makkah that I may invite them to Islam." No sooner had the Prophet sent him than he called him back saying, "Bring my uncle back to me, that the 'polytheists' may not kill him." Al-'Abbas, however, refused to return until he came to Makkah and made the following statement: "O ye people, embrace Islam and ye shall be*

---

[175] *The History of al-Tabari: The Victory of Islam*, p. 171. There was a similar report from another source:

> *When the apostle camped at Marr al-Zahran 'Abbas said, 'Alas, Quraysh, if the apostle enters Mecca by force before they come and ask for protection that will be the end of Quraysh for ever.*

*The Life of Muhammad (Sirat Rasul Allah)*, p. 546.

*safe. Ye have been surrounded on all sides. Ye are*
*confronted by a hard case that is beyond your power.*
*Here is Khalid in the lower part of Makkah, there is az-*
*Zubair in the upper part of it, and there is the Prophet of*
*Allah at the head of the Emigrants, Ansar and*
*Khuza'ah.* "[176]

After al-'Abbas had returned, Abu Sufyan bin Harith, a Meccan non-
Muslim and a cousin of Muhammad, approached the Muslim camp:

> *...Abu Sufyan along with Hakim bin Hizam and Budail bin*
> *Warqa', two terrible polytheists, went out to survey.*
> *Before they got near the camp, they met 'Abbas, the*
> *Prophet's uncle. He informed Abu Sufyan of the situation*
> *and advised him to accept Islam and persuade his people*
> *to surrender before Muhammad; otherwise, his head*
> *would be struck off.*[177]

Abu Sufyan was given protection by al-'Abbas. But the threat to cut off
Abu Sufyan's head almost became a reality when al-'Abbas brought him
in front of Muhammad the next morning. Muhammad asked Abu Sufyan

---

[176]     *The Origins of the Islamic State*, p. 63.

[177]     *The Sealed Nectar*, p. 462. There were two other reports about the
content of the initial comments between al-'Abbas and Abu Sufyan:

> *Abu Sufyan said, "What brings you?" Al-'Abbas said, "This is*
> *the Messenger of God with ten thousand Muslims. So convert!"*

*The Life of Muhammad: Al-Waqidi's Kitab al-Maghazi*, p. 401.

> *He* [Abu Sufyan] *said: I am here, what is behind you? He* [al-
> 'Abbas] *said: It is the Apostle of Allah with ten thousand strong.*
> *Embrace Islam, may your mother and tribe be berieved* [sic] *of*
> *you.*

*Kitab al-Tabaqat al-Kabir*, Vol. 2, p. 167.

to acknowledge that there was only one god, Allah; Abu Sufyan did so. But then uncertainty on Abu Sufyan's part became a factor; Muhammad said,

> Woe to you Abu Sufyan! Is it not time that you
> acknowledge me as Allah's Prophet and Messenger?"
> Abu Sufyan said, "I still have some doubt as to that."
> Abbas intervened saying, "Embrace Islam before you lose
> your head." Abu Sufyan then recited the confession of
> faith and thus he entered Islam.[178]

So when threatened in the presence of Muhammad with having his head cut off, Abu Sufyan resolved his uncertainty about Muhammad's status as Allah's Prophet and Messenger, and he became a Muslim.

After this, Abu Sufyan stood with al-'Abbas and watched thousands of Muslim warriors marching toward Mecca. Fearing that his fellow Meccans would be killed by the Muslims if they resisted, Abu Sufyan rushed ahead to Mecca and called for the Meccans to surrender to the Muslim army.

There were various reports about what Abu Sufyan told the Meccans, but the underlying theme of all these reports was that the Meccans would soon be confronted by a formidable, hostile Muslim force, and the only way they could save themselves would be by converting to Islam or seeking refuge in Abu Sufyan's house.

---

[178] *When the Moon Split*, p. 326. For additional reports about Abu Sufyan being brought into the presence of Muhammad and given the choice of converting to Islam or having his head cut off, see: *The History of al-Tabari: The Victory of Islam*, p. 173; *The Life of Muhammad (Sirat Rasul Allah)*, p. 547; and *Abridged Biography of Prophet Muhammad*, p. 256. For a report that while in the presence of Muhammad Abu Sufyan was given the choice of converting to Islam or simply being "killed," see *The Life of Muhammad: Al-Waqidi's Kitab al-Maghazi*, p. 403.

> *Abu Sufyan exclaimed, "March on, 'Abbas, for never*
> *before today have I seen a people so ready for war and so*
> *arrayed in their tribes. Abu Sufyan left after that, and*
> *when he could look out over Mecca, he cried out using the*
> *war cry of the Quraysh, "O Victorious People! Surrender*
> *as Muslims, that you may be saved!" His wife Hind then*
> *came out to join him, but grabbing hold of his beard, cried*
> *out, "O Victorious People! Kill the old fool! He's*
> *abandoned his religion!" Abu Sufyan replied, "I swear by*
> *the One in Whose hand my soul resides, you will be a*
> *Muslim or have your head severed from your neck!"[179]*

## *The Life of Muhammad: Al-Waqidi's Kitab al-Maghazi*

> *And he began to call out in Mecca, "O people of the*
> *Quraysh, woe unto you! Indeed he has brought what was*
> *out of your reach! This is Muhammad with ten thousand,*
> *wearing iron, so submit!" They said, "May God*
> *denounce you as the delegate of the people!" Hind began*
> *to say, "Kill this delegate of yours! May God denounce*
> *you as the delegate of the people!"...Abu Sufyan said,*
> *"Woe unto you, this woman shall not deceive you from*
> *yourselves! I saw what you did not see! I saw the men,*
> *the quivers, and the weapons. One has no strength for*
> *this!"[180]*

---

[179]    *The Expeditions (Kitab al-Maghazi)*, pp. 99-101.

[180]    *The Life of Muhammad: Al-Waqidi's Kitab al-Maghazi*, p. 405.

> *When he came to them he cried at the top of his voice: 'O Quraysh, this is Muhammad who has come to you with a force you cannot resist. He who enters Abu Sufyan's house is safe.' Hind d. 'Utba went up to him, and seizing his moustaches cried, 'Kill this fat greasy bladder of lard! What a rotten protector of the people!' He said, 'Woe to you, don't let this woman deceive you, for you cannot resist what has come.'*[181]

*Abridged Biography of Prophet Muhammad*

> *Abu Sufyan then went on to Makkah and when he reached Quraish, he shouted in his loudest voice: "This is Muhammad who has come to you with forces which you can never resist, so whoever enters the house of Abu Sufyan will be safe."*[182]

*The History of al-Tabari: The Victory of Islam*

> *Abu Sufyan departed in haste. When he reached Mecca, he shouted in the sanctuary, "People of Quraysh, behold Muhammad has come upon you with forces you cannot resist...Anyone who enters my house will be safe."*[183]

---

[181]  *The Life of Muhammad (Sirat Rasul Allah)*, p. 548.

[182]  *Abridged Biography of Prophet Muhammad*, p. 257.

[183]  *The History of al-Tabari: The Victory of Islam*, p. 174.

> *...Abu Sufyan hurried back to Makkah and announced*
> *loudly: "O people of the Quraysh, this is Muhammad who*
> *has come to you with an army you cannot resist.*[184]

As the Muslim army advanced on Mecca,

> *the Quraysh assembled some of their men...and entrusted*
> *them with the last sign of resistance against the Muslim*
> *army. If they too fell, there was no choice but to accept*
> *the Muslim supremacy over Makkah. And indeed that day*
> *there was no choice before the Quraysh but to accept*
> *Allah's decree...Allah's Messenger would finally enter*
> *His Sacred Mosque, victorious and unchallenged.*[185]

Ibn Kathir wrote that the conquest of Mecca "was a forcible conquest by the Prophet,"[186] which resulted in "some deaths" among the non-Muslim Meccans.[187]

Abu Hurairah reported that Muhammad had given a special order to the *Ansar*:

> *The Messenger of Allah (may peace be upon him) said (to*
> *the Ansar): You see the ruffians and the (lowly) followers*
> *of Quraish. And he indicated by (striking) one of his*
> *hands over the other that they should be killed and said:*
> *Meet me at As-Safa' [a hill]. Then we went on (and) if any*

---

184    *When the Moon Split*, p. 327.

185    Ibid., p. 328.

186    *Tafsir Ibn Kathir*, Part 2, p. 117.

187    *Tafsir Ibn Kathir*, Vol. 1, p. 529.

*one of us wanted that a certain person should be killed, he was killed, and no one could resist.*[188]

Muhammad gave a similar order to one of his commanders:

> *The Messenger of Allah continued on his way, until he entered Makkah from above and he ordered Khalid bin Al-Waleed to enter it from below and he said: "If any of Quraish opposes you, kill him and proceed until you meet me at As-Safa." And none opposed them without being killed.*[189]

Ibn Sa'd wrote:

> *The Apostle of Allah, may Allah bless him, forced his entry into Makkah. Then the people embraced Islam willingly or unwillingly.*[190]

---

[188] *Sahih Muslim*, Vol. 5, No. 1780, p. 201. The *Ansar* were the Muslims who were native to Medina. For a similar report by Abu Hurairah in which Muhammad said to the *Ansar*, "Go this way, and whoever appears before you, kill him", see *Sunan Abu Dawud*, Vol. 3, No. 3024, p. 513. At-Tamimi reported Abu Hurairah's narration with slightly different wording:

> *The Messenger of Allah said: "O Abu Hurairah!" I replied: "Here I am at your service, O Messenger of Allah!" He said: "Call the Ansar for me and do not bring me anyone who is not an Ansari." So I called them and the Messenger of Allah came and they encircled him and he said to them: "Do you see the forces of Quraish and their followers?" Then he said, placing one hand over the other: "Wipe them out and then meet me at As-Safa." Abu Hurairah said: "So we left and each of us killed as many of them as he wished..."*

*Abridged Biography of Prophet Muhammad*, p. 259.

[189] *Abridged Biography of Prophet Muhammad*, p. 257.

[190] *Kitab al-Tabaqat al-Kabir*, Vol. 2, p. 168.

And after the conquest of Mecca,

> *the Makkans came to realize that the only way to success
> lay in the avenue of Islam. They complied with the new
> realities and gathered to pledge loyalty to the Prophet.*[191]

So the non-Muslims of Mecca

> *gathered together in Mecca to do homage to the apostle in
> Islam...he sat (waiting) from them on al-Safa while 'Umar
> remained below him imposing conditions on the people
> who paid homage to the apostle promising to hear and
> obey God and His apostle to the best of their ability.*[192]

Prior to the actual entry into Mecca, Muhammad had ordered nine people, including four women, to be killed; four or five of these nine were captured and killed. The others saved themselves by converting to Islam before they could be killed. In terms of lives lost during the battle for Mecca, there were estimates that the Meccans lost 12-13 men and the Muslims lost three.[193]

---

[191]     *The Sealed Nectar*, p. 470.

[192]     *The Life of Muhammad (Sirat Rasul Allah)*, p. 553.

[193]     Ibid., pp. 549-551. For similar reports about the violence that occurred when the Muslims conquered Mecca, see, e.g., *The History of al-Tabari: The Victory of Islam*, pp. 177-181; *The Expeditions (Kitab al-Maghazi)*, p. 101; *Kitab al-Tabaqat al-Kabir*, Vol. 2, p. 168; *Abridged Biography of Prophet Muhammad*, pp. 257-259; *The Life of Muhammad: Al-Waqidi's Kitab al-Maghazi*, pp. 406-408, 413, 415, and 421-424; and 'Imaduddeen Isma'eel ibn Katheer al-Qurashi, *Winning the Hearts and Souls: Expeditions and Delegations in the Lifetime of Prophet Muhammad*, trans. Research Department of Darussalam (Riyadh, Kingdom of Saudi Arabia: Darussalam, 2010), pp. 46-48, and 55.

It is interesting that this information about the violent conquest of Mecca from our early authoritative sources directly contradicts many modern writings that describe the conquest of Mecca as a peaceful undertaking (e.g., Ingrid Mattson, *The Story of the Qur'an, Its History and Place in Muslim Life* (West Sussex, UK:

After the conquest of Mecca, Muhammad said,

> *If anyone should say, 'The apostle killed men in Mecca,*
> *say God permitted His apostle to do so but He does not*
> *permit you.*[194]

Immediately after the conquest of Mecca, Muhammad began sending out Muslim forces to attack those who were not following Islam.[195]

## January 630 – An "Invitation" to the Banu Jadhima

Muhammad sent a 350 man detachment under Khalid bin al-Walid to invite the Banu Jadhimah to Islam. When confronted, the Banu Jadhimah said they were already Muslims and laid down their weapons. The Muslims bound them and later beheaded many of them because Khalid did not think they were really Muslims. When Muhammad heard about this, he sent an envoy to pay "blood money" and compensation for property that had been taken.[196]

---

John Wiley and Sons, Ltd., 2013), p. 68; and Karen Armstrong, *Islam, A Short History* (New York: Modern Library Edition, 2000), p. 23).

[194]     *The Life of Muhammad (Sirat Rasul Allah)*, p. 555.

[195]     *The Life of Muhammad: Al-Waqidi's Kitab al-Maghazi*, p. 429.

[196]     In *The Sealed Nectar*, a 20th century award-winning biography of Muhammad, this "invitation to Islam" was noted, but there was no mention of the fact that the Banu Jadhimah had claimed that they were already Muslims; Khalid's actions towards them were explained in this way:

> *He was instructed to carry out his mission with peace and*
> *goodwill. There, the people were not articulate enough to*
> *communicate their intentions, so Khalid ordered his men to kill*
> *them and take the others as captives. He even had in mind to*
> *kill the captives but some of the Companions were opposed to*
> *his plan. News of the bloodshed reached the Prophet. He was*
> *deeply grieved and raised his hands towards the heaven,*

However, it was reported that Khalid later explained,

*I did not fight until 'Abdallah b. Hudhafah al-Sahmi*
*commanded me to do so. He said, 'The Messenger of God*

---

*uttering these words: "O Allah! I am innocent of what Khalid*
*has done," twice.*

*The Sealed Nectar*, p. 472. Two *hadiths* from *Sahih Al-Bukhari* were cited as support for this story. However, as we can see from examining those two particular *hadiths*, there was actually no mention in them that Khalid *was instructed to carry out his mission with peace and goodwill*:

*Narrated Salim's father: The Prophet sent Khalid bin Al-Walid*
*to the tribe of Jadhima; and Khalid invited them to Islam but*
*they could not express themselves by saying: "Aslamna (i.e., we*
*have embraced Islam)," but they started saying: "Saba'na!*
*Saba'na (i.e., we have come out of one religion to another)."*
*Khalid kept on killing (some of) them and taking (some of) them*
*as captives...*

*Sahih Al-Bukhari*, Vol. 5, Book 64, No. 4339, p. 381; the title for this *hadith* was "The Prophet sent Khalid bin-Al-Walid (to fight) with Banu Jadhima."

Here is the second *hadith* cited in *The Sealed Nectar*:

*Narrated Ibn 'Umar: The Prophet sent (an army unit under the*
*command of) Khalid bin Al-Walid to fight against the tribe of*
*Bani Jadhima and those people could not express themselves by*
*saying, "Aslamna," but they said, "Saba'na! Saba'na!" Khalid*
*kept on killing some of them and taking some others as*
*captives...*

*Sahih Al-Bukhari*, Vol. 9, Book 93, No. 7189, p. 188; Footnote No. 3 for this *hadith* pointed out:

*Khalid killed those people because he thought that they should*
*have expressed their conversion to Islam explicitly by saying,*
*"Aslamna!".*

*has commanded you to kill them because of their resistance to Islam.'"*[197]

This explanation by Khalid was supported by a report from ibn Sa'd that Muhammad had given a general command to kill anyone who was not a Muslim:

> *Al-'Abbas Ibn al-Fadl informed us, Sufyan Ibn 'Uyaynah informed us: 'Abd al-Malik Ibn Nawfal Ibn Musahiq al-Qurashi related to me on the authority of his father; he said: The Apostle of Allah, may Allah bless him, sent us on the day of Nakhlah (when al-'Uzza was demolished), and said: Slay the people as long as you do not hear a mu'adhdhin* [one who calls Muslims to prayer] *or see a mosque.*[198]

## January 630 – Convert and Get Your Family Returned

Muhammad now led a force of 12,000 Muslims against the Hawazin and Thaqif tribes. They battled at the valley of Hunayn and the Muslims were initially put to flight. However, they were able to rally and then defeat the Hawazin and Thaqif; the women, children and flocks of these tribes were divided among the Muslims.

After the battle, Muhammad inquired about one of the tribal leaders who was absent. Muhammad offered to return that leader's family and property if that leader became a Muslim; the leader did so:

> *The apostle asked the Hawazin deputation about Malik b. 'Auf and they said that he was in al-Ta'if with Thaqif. The apostle told them to tell Malik that if he came to him as a*

---

[197]     *The History of al-Tabari: The Victory of Islam*, p. 190. This explanation by Khalid was also reported in *The Life of Muhammad (Sirat Rasul Allah)*, p. 562.

[198]     *Kitab al-Tabaqat al-Kabir*, Vol. 2, p. 184.

*Muslim he would return his family and property to him*
*and give him a hundred camels. On hearing this Malik*
*came out from al-Ta'if...and rode off to join the*
*apostle...He gave him back his family and property and*
*gave him a hundred camels. He became an excellent*
*Muslim...[199]*


## February-March 630 - Muhammad's letter to Oman

During this time Muhammad sent a letter to the King of Oman and the
King's brother. He said that if they "embrace Islam" they would remain in
charge of their country; otherwise all of their possessions were
"perishable":

*Peace be upon him who follows true guidance; thereafter*
*I invite both of you to the Call of Islam. Embrace*
*Islam...If you two accept Islam, you will remain in*
*command of your country; but if you refuse my Call, you*
*must remember that all your possessions are perishable.*
*My cavalry would take possession of your land, and my*
*Prophethood will assume superiority over your*
*kingship.[200]*

---

[199]     *The Life of Muhammad (Sirat Rasul Allah)*, p. 593. This offer by
Muhammad was also reported in *The History of al-Tabari: The Last Years of the
Prophet*, p. 30; *The Life of Muhammad: Al-Waqidi's Kitab al-Maghazi*, p. 467;
*Winning the Hearts and Souls: Expeditions and Delegations in the Lifetime of
Prophet Muhammad*, p. 104; and *Kitab al-Tabaqat al-Kabir*, Vol. 1, p. 369.

[200]     *The Sealed Nectar*, p. 424; this incident is reported to have occurred
sometime after the January 630 conquest of Mecca (*The Sealed Nectar*, p. 426;
and *When the Moon Split*, p. 290). Ibn Sa'd wrote that it occurred in February-
March of 630 (*Kitab al-Tabaqat al-Kabir*, Vol. 1, p. 309). Al-Tabari noted more
generally that this incident occurred sometime in 8 AH (May 1, 629 – April 19,
630) – see *The History of al-Tabari: The Victory of Islam*, p. 142. However, al-
Baladhuri wrote that this incident occurred in the early part of the year 8 of the

Muhammad's emissary, Amr bin Aas, summed up the situation to them:

> *...if you embrace Islam, you will be safe, or else our cavalry will trample your land and wipe out its greenery.*[201]

The king and his brother accepted Islam.

## March 630 – We Convert, So Call Back Your Army

Muhammad sent a force of 400 Muslim warriors to the territory of al-Yaman and ordered them "to devastate Suda."[202]

Ziyad ibn al-Harith as-Suda'i, one of the people of Suda, learned about the approaching Muslim army and rushed to see Muhammad. Ziyad said:

> *"I came to Allah's Messenger, peace and blessings of Allah be upon him, and I gave him the pledge of Islam. I informed him that he had dispatched an army to fight my*

---

Islamic Calendar (8 AH), which would be around May-June of 629 – *The Origins of the Islamic* State, p. 116.

There were four main tasks for the Muslim cavalry units:

1. Protect the outskirts of Medina;
2. Intercept Meccan trade caravans;
3. Make covenants with other tribes outside Medina;
4. "Lastly, the units were entrusted with the task of spreading the message of Islam throughout Arabia."

*When the Moon Split*, p. 188. The Muslim cavalry units were the armed apostles of Islam.

[201]    *When the Moon Split*, p. 291.

[202]    *Kitab al-Tabaqat al-Kabir*, Vol. 1, p. 384.

*people so I said to him: 'Allah's Messenger, bring back
the army and I give you the promise of my people's
acceptance of Islam and their obedience.'*[203]

Muhammad ordered the Muslim army to return, and the people of Suda
accepted Islam.

[203]    *Winning the Hearts and Souls: Expeditions and Delegations in the
Lifetime of Prophet Muhammad*, p. 209; for a similar narration see: *Kitab al-
Tabaqat al-Kabir*, Vol. 1, pp. 384-385; and *The Sealed Nectar*, p. 520.

# The Year of the Deputations – 9 AH

*He enkindled the fire of holy war, he led the horses to the battle-field, going ahead when the fire of fighting was burning intensely.*[204]

The Year 9 AH of the Muslim calendar covered the time period of April 20, 630 to April 8, 631. Muslim historians designated this year as *The Year of the Deputations*. During this year representatives of Arab tribes started coming to Medina to accept Islam. But many of these representatives were not coming to accept Islam willingly. Ibn Ishaq explained the reason for this growing acceptance of Islam:

> *In deciding their attitude to Islam the Arabs were only waiting to see what happened to this clan of Quraysh and the apostle. For Quraysh were the leaders and guides of men, the people of the sacred temple* [the Ka'bah], *and the pure stock of Ishmael son of Abraham; and the leading Arabs did not contest this. It was Quraysh who had declared war on the apostle and opposed him; and when Mecca was occupied and Quraysh became subject to him and he subdued it to Islam, and the Arabs knew that they could not fight the apostle or display enmity towards him they entered into God's religion 'in batches' as God said, coming to him from all directions.*[205]

---

[204]      From Hassan ibn Thabit's elegy to Muhammad, *Kitab al-Tabaqat al-Kabir*, Vol. 2, p. 409.

[205]      *The Life of Muhammad (Sirat Rasul Allah)*, p. 628. This "practical" attitude of the Arabs was also noted in *Winning the Hearts and Souls: Expeditions*

This rush by Arab tribes to convert to Islam even resulted in a young boy becoming the *imam* (in this case, the prayer leader) of his tribe:

> *Narrated 'Amr bin Salama...So, when Makkah was conquered, then every tribe rushed to embrace Islam, and my father hurried to embrace Islam before (the other members of) my tribe. When my father returned (from the Prophet) to his tribe, he said, "By Allah, I have come to you from the Prophet for sure!" The Prophet afterwards said to them, "...and let the one amongst you who knows the Qur'an most should [sic] lead the Salat (prayer)." So they looked for such a person and found none who knew more of the Qur'an than I because of the Quranic verses which I used to learn from the caravans. They therefore made me their Imam [to lead the Salat (prayer)] and at that time I was a boy of six or seven years..."[206]*

## Muhammad's Letters to Arab Leaders

It was during this year that Muhammad sent numerous written messages to the leaders of many of the Arab tribes.

For example, some members of the Banu Lakhm tribe had "embraced Islam on the basis of mere guess," and as long as they stayed Muslim they would be protected by Allah and Muhammad. But there would be no such protection for those who left Islam and returned to their old religion:

> *The Apostle of Allah, may Allah bless him, wrote to those from among the Banu Lakhm, who had embraced Islam on*

---

*and Delegations in the Lifetime of Prophet Muhammad*, p. 165; and *Abridged Biography of Prophet Muhammad*, p. 301.

[206]   *Sahih Al-Bukhari*, Vol. 5, Book 64, No. 4302, pp. 359-360. This was also reported in *Sunan Abu Dawud*, Vol. 1, No. 585, p. 359; *Sunan An-Nasa'i*, Vol. 1, No. 790, p. 466; and *Kitab al-Tabaqat al-Kabir*, Vol. 1, pp. 396-397.

*the basis of mere guess, used to offer prayers, pay zakah
and the share of Allah and His Apostle and had
abandoned the polytheists, that they were safe under the
guarantee of Allah and the guarantee of Muhammad that
from him who would return to his old religion the
guarantee of Allah and the guarantee of Muhammad His
Apostle, would be withdrawn, but, if a Muslim bore
witness to his Islam, he would be safe under the guarantee
of Allah and the guarantee of His Apostle.*[207]

And in other correspondence during this time period, we find Muhammad
1) extending a guarantee of protection and the retention of land and
property to 16 Arab tribes, and 2) promising 11 individual tribal leaders
that they would retain the land and property they possessed when they
converted to Islam, all on the condition that they remained Muslims.[208]

---

[207]     *Kitab al-Tabaqat al-Kabir*, Vol. 1, p. 315.

[208]     Ibid., pp. 315-321, 325, 331, 337, 339, 340, and 357.

Tribes:  1) Banu al-Dibab; 2) Banu Ziyad Ibn al-Harith; 3) Banu al-Harith; 4)
Banu Nahd; 5) Banu Qanan Ibn Yazid; 6) Banu Mu'awiyah Ibn Jarwal; 7) Banu
Juwayn; 8) Banu Ma'n; 9) Banu Ju'ayl; 10) Banu Jurmuz Ibn Rabi'ah; 11) Banu
al-Huraqah; 12) Banu al-Jurmuz; 13) Banu Ghifar; 14) Banu Wa'il; 15) Banu
Khath'am; and 16) Banu 'Uqayl.

It is interesting to note that with regard to the Banu Khath'am, Muhammad stated
that his guarantee extended to "whoever embraces Islam willingly or
unwillingly…" (p. 339).

Individual Tribal Leaders: 1) Khalid Ibn Dimad al-Azdi; 2)Yazid Ibn al-Tufayl al-
Harithi; 3) 'Abd Yaghuth Ibn Wa'lah al-Harithi; 4) Dhu al-Ghussah Qays Ibn al-
Husayn; 5) 'Amir Ibn al-Aswad Ibn 'Amir Ibn Juwayn al-Ta'i; 6) Junadah al-
Azdi; 7) 'Amr Ibn Ma'bad al-Juhni; 8) Habib Ibn 'Amr; 9) Nahshal Ibn Malik al-
Wa'ili; 10) Mahra Ibn al-Abyad; and 11) Wa'il Ibn Hujr.

Muhammad even offered Arab tribal land to a Christian leader if he converted to Islam:

> *The Apostle of Allah, may Allah bless him, wrote to Ma'di Karib Ibn Abrahah that the land of Khawlan will be his if he embraced Islam.*[209]

And during this time, Muhammad sent a letter to the ruler and the people of Najran "inviting" them to convert to Islam, pay the *Jizyah*, or fight:

> *"In the Name of the God of Ibrahim, Ishaq and Ya'qoob. From Muhammad, Allah's Messenger, to the prelate and to the people of Najran; if you accept Islam then I will give praise to the God of Ibrahim, Ishaq and Ya'qoob. I am inviting you to the worship of Allah away from the worship of slaves; I invite you to the Authority of Allah away from the authority of slaves. However, if you decline, then it is incumbent on you to pay the Jizyah. If you reject, then I warn you of a war."*[210]

In response to this letter, a delegation from Najran was sent to see Muhammad. The people of Najran subsequently decided to pay a *Jizyah* of "two thousand suits of garments."[211] They also agreed that if there was a conflict between the Muslims and non-Muslim tribes in the area, the people of Najran would loan the Muslims thirty coats of armor, thirty spears, thirty camels, and thirty steeds.[212]

---

[209]    *Kitab al-Tabaqat al-Kabir*, Vol. 1, p. 314.

[210]    *Winning the Hearts and Souls: Expeditions and Delegations in the Lifetime of Prophet Muhammad*, p. 177.

[211]    Ibid., p. 181.

[212]    *Kitab al-Tabaqat al-Kabir*, Vol. 1, p. 419. This *Jizyah* payment was also mentioned in *The Origins of the Islamic State*, pp. 98 and 100.

Muhammad offered another tribe the option of paying the *Jizyah* in order to maintain peace with the Muslims:

> *The Apostle of Allah, may Allah bless him, wrote: In the name of Allah, the Beneficent, the Merciful. This is an epistle from Muhammad, the Apostle of Allah, to Banu Ghadiya. They have to guarantee the payment of the jizyah in return (for a guarantee from us that) there will be no oppression on them, nor banishment.*[213]

For yet another tribe, the offer of safety from Muhammad was contingent on them converting to Islam, disassociating themselves from non-Muslims, and paying one-fifth of their plunder to Muhammad:

> *In the name of Allah, the Beneficent, the Merciful. From Muhammad, the Prophet, to Banu Zuhayr Ibn Uqaysh, a sub-tribe of 'Ukal. If they bear witness to, (the formula that) there is no god save Allah and that Muhammad is the Apostle of Allah, they dissociate themselves with the polytheists and promise to pay one-fifth of their booty as the general and particular shares of the Prophet, they will be safe under the protection of Allah and His Apostle.*[214]

And during this *Year of the Deputations*, Muhammad sent numerous military expeditions against other non-Muslim tribes.

## April 630 – Killing Non-Muslims is a Small Matter

Muhammad sent 50 Muslim horsemen against the Banu Tamim, who had urged other tribes not to pay the *Jizyah* to the Muslims. The Muslims

---

[213]    *Kitab al-Tabaqat al-Kabir*, Vol. 1, p. 330.

[214]    Ibid.

attacked, captured many prisoners (including women and children), and returned to Medina.

When the delegation from the Banu Tamim subsequently arrived in Medina, they challenged Muhammad to a "boasting" competition. After the Banu Tamim's poet had finished, Muhammad said to Thabit b. Qays,

> "Get up and answer the man's speech'; so Thabit got up and said: '...We are God's helpers and the assistants of His apostle, and will fight men until they believe in God; and he who believes in God and His apostle has protected his life and property from us; and he who disbelieves we will fight in God unceasingly and killing him will be a small matter to us.[215]

---

[215] *The Life of Muhammad (Sirat Rasul Allah)*, p. 629. Similar wording was reported in *The History of al-Tabari: The Last Years of the Prophet*, p. 69:

> ...we fight people until they believe in God. He who believes in God and His Messenger has protected his life and possessions [from us]; as for one who disbelieves, we will fight him forever in the cause of God and killing him is a small matter for us.

Also in *The Life of Muhammad: Al-Waqidi's Kitab al-Maghazi*, p. 478:

> We are the Ansar – the helpers – of God and His Messenger. We fight the people until they say, 'There is but one God.' The property and blood of those who believe in God and His Messenger are forbidden. Who disbelieves in God, we will fight him about that. His death is easy.

And in *Abridged Biography of Prophet Muhammad*, pp. 304-305, where Thabit talked about supporting and sheltering Muhammad, and then he continued,

> And we fought the people with sharp swords, until they followed his religion...If you have come to protect your lives and your property, then swear by Allah that you will not associate any partner with Allah, and embrace Islam...

So in Muhammad's presence Thabit bragged that the Muslims would fight non-Muslims until they converted to Islam, and only then would they be safe. And if they did not convert, killing them would "be a small matter" to the Muslims. There is no record that Muhammad disagreed with this statement.

When the "boasting" competition was finished, the Banu Tamim accepted Islam. Afterwards,

> [t]he Prophet's work continued. He tried to make as many people accept Islam as he could. Using his words, his generosity, and last of all, physical strength, he tried to convince them of the truth.[216]

## June 630 – An "Invitation" to the Banu Kilab

Muslim fighters were sent to the Banu Kilab to "invite" them to Islam:

> This mission was sent to Bani Kilab to call them to embrace Islam. Refusing to embrace Islam, they started to fight against the Muslims, but were defeated and one man was killed.[217]

The one man who was killed was the non-Muslim father of one of the Muslim warriors:

> They (narrators) said: The Apostle of Allah, may Allah bless him, sent a force…against [the Banu Kilab]…They encountered them at al-Zujj…and invited them to embrace Islam. They refused, so they attacked them and forced them to flee. Then al-Asyad met his father Salamah who

---

216      *When the Moon Split*, p. 352.

217      *The Sealed Nectar*, p. 491.

*was on his own horse, in a pond of al-Zujj. He invited his
father to embrace Islam promising him amnesty. He
(father) abused him and his creed. Consequently al-Asyad
hamstrung the horse of his father. When the horse fell on
its hoofs, Salamah reclined on his spear in water. He (al-
Asyad) held him till one of them (Muslims) came there and
killed him. His son did not kill him.*[218]


## July 630 – Refer All Differences to Muhammad

4:59 of the Koran was "revealed" at this time about the Muslim
commander of the Expedition to Habasha.[219] Here is that verse:

> *O you who believe! Obey Allah and obey the Messenger
> (Muhammad), and those of you (Muslims) who are in
> authority. (And) if you differ in anything amongst
> yourselves, refer it to Allah and His Messenger, if you
> believe in Allah and in the Last Day. That is better and
> more suitable for final determination.*

---

[218]     *Kitab al-Tabaqat al-Kabir*, Vol. 2, p. 201. This incident was also
reported in *The Life of Muhammad: Al-Waqidi's Kitab al-Maghazi*, p. 481.

[219]     *Tafsir Ibn Kathir*, Vol. 2, p. 495; *Al-Wahidi's Asbab al-Nuzul*, p. 76;
*Sahih Muslim*, Vol. 6, No. 1834, p. 248; *Sahih Al-Bukhari*, Vol. 6, Book 65, No.
4584, p. 93; and *Jami' At-Tirmidhi*, Vol. 3, No. 1672, p. 417.

Ibn Kathir's description of this military expedition matched the descriptions of
such an expedition mentioned in *Kitab al-Tabaqat al-Kabir*, Vol. 2, pp. 201-202,
and *The Life of Muhammad: Al-Waqidi's Kitab al-Maghazi*, p. 482. The date of
Rabi' al-Akhir 9 (July 630) for this expedition was specifically mentioned by ibn
Sa'd, and implied by its chronological listing by al-Waqidi. As a side note, Ibn
Ishaq mentioned this incident in the time frame of "The Attack of Dhu Qarad,"
which occurred around August 627 - *The Life of Muhammad (Sirat Rasul Allah)*,
pp. 486 and 677.

So the Muslims were again commanded to obey Allah and to obey Muhammad, and any disagreements were to be referred to Allah and Muhammad. Since Muhammad was the only one who spoke for Allah, this meant that all differences were to be referred to Muhammad.

## July 630 – To the Captives: Convert or Die

Muhammad sent 150 warriors under the command of Ali bin Abi Talib to the land of Tayyi' to demolish an idol named al-Fuls. There were many captives taken during this expedition. The Muslim warriors offered the captives a chance to convert to Islam. Those captives who converted were spared, those who refused were killed:

> *When the dawn rose, they raided and killed those who were killed and took prisoners. They drove the children and women and gathered the sheep and cattle... The* [Muslim] *soldiers came and gathered. They came close to the prisoners and offered them Islam. Those who converted were left, and those who refused were executed...* [220]

There is no record that Muhammad disagreed with these actions.

## October 630 - Muhammad's Letter to Heraclius

Muhammad led an army of 30,000 Muslims against the Byzantines (this was known as the *Ghazwah* of Tabuk). The Muslims went to Tabuk, waited several days, and then returned to Medina. There was no contact with the Byzantines.

---

[220]     *The Life of Muhammad: Al-Waqidi's Kitab al-Maghazi*, p. 484.

But while in Tabuk, Muhammad sent a messenger with a letter to Heraclius, the Emperor of Byzantium; in this letter Muhammad offered Heraclius the option of converting to Islam, paying the *Jizyah*, or fighting:

> *Certainly, Allah's Messenger, peace and blessings of Allah be upon him, arrived at Tabook and sent Dihyah Al-Kalbi to Heraclius. When the letter of Allah's Messenger reached him, he invited the vicars and the Roman patriarchs and then locked the door behind them. He addressed them saying: A letter has reached me from this man, as you have seen, inviting me to one of three choices: follow his religion, give him our wealth from our land even though the land belongs to us, or to confront him in battle. By Allah you are well aware from what you have read in the Divine Book that he will conquer whatever is under my feet, therefore come, so that we may follow his religion or give him the wealth of our land.[221]*

As Heraclius put it, paying the *Jizyah* would save them from Muhammad's military forces:

> *Come and I will pay him the poll-tax every year and avert his onslaught and get rest from war by the money I pay him.[222]*

It was also reported that Heraclius said:

> *...let me give him tribute each year, so that I can avert his vehemence from me and find rest from his warfare by means of money that I give to him.[223]*

---

[221]   *Winning the Hearts and Souls: Expeditions and Delegations in the Lifetime of Prophet Muhammad*, p. 130. A shorter version of this was reported in *The Life of Muhammad (Sirat Rasul Allah)*, p. 656.

[222]   *The Life of Muhammad (Sirat Rasul Allah)*, p. 657.

[223]   *The History of al-Tabari: The Victory of Islam*, p. 107.

Heraclius' advisers refused to convert and refused to pay the *Jizyah*, and Muhammad did not lead any more Muslim forces against the Byzantines.

It was about this time that Koran Verses 9:63, 9:71, 9:73, and 9:123 were "revealed."[224] Verses 9:63 and 9:71 were commands to the Muslims to obey Allah and Muhammad, and advised them that the "fire of Hell" would be waiting for those who refused.

## October 630 – Verse 9:73 Abrogates 2:256

But we also have a verse in which, according to ibn 'Abbas, Allah commanded Muhammad "to fight the disbelievers with the sword":

Chapter 9, Verse 73

> *O Prophet (Muhammad)! Strive hard against the disbelievers and the hypocrites, and be harsh against them, their abode is Hell, - and worst indeed is that destination.*

Ibn Kathir explained this verse in a section titled *The Order for Jihad against the Disbelievers and Hypocrites*:

> *Allah commanded His Messenger to strive hard against the disbelievers and the hypocrites and to be harsh against them...Ibn 'Abbas said, "Allah commanded the Prophet to fight the disbelievers with the sword, to strive against the hypocrites with the tongue and annulled lenient treatment of them." Ad-Dahhak commented, "Perform Jihad against the disbelievers with the sword..."*[225]

---

[224]     *The Life of Muhammad: Al-Waqidi's Kitab al-Maghazi*, pp. 522-523, and 526. Pickthall included Verses 9:63, 9:71, and 9:73 as among those "revealed" about the Tabuk campaign - see *The Meaning of the Glorious Koran*, p. 191.

[225]     *Tafsir Ibn Kathir*, Vol. 4, pp. 474-475.

The *Tafsir Al-Jalalayn* reiterated the idea of fighting the disbelievers with the sword:

> **O Prophet, do jihad against the unbelievers** *with the sword...*[226]

And there was a similar explanation in the *Tafsir Ibn 'Abbas*:

> *(O Prophet! Strive against the disbelievers) with the sword...*[227]

Al-Qurtubi pointed out that many Muslim scholars believed that 9:73 had actually abrogated 2:256:

> *It is said that it is abrogated because the Prophet, may Allah bless him and grant him peace, forced the Arabs to adopt the din* [religion] *of Islam and fought them and was only pleased with Islam for them. Sulayman ibn Musa took that view, saying "It is abrogated by 'O Prophet! Do jihad against the unbelievers and the hypocrites.' (9:73)" That is related from Ibn Mas'ud and many commentators.*[228]

Ibn Kathir listed verses 9:73 and 9:123 after 48:16 when he had noted that 2:256 had been abrogated by "the verse of 'Fighting [48:16].'"[229] The implication was that 9:73 and 9:123 had also abrogated 2:256. The fact that 2:256 had been abrogated was boldly stated by ibn Kathir in the next paragraph:

---

[226]     *Tafsir Al-Jalalayn*, p. 419.

[227]     *Tafsir Ibn 'Abbas*, p. 240.

[228]     *Tafsir Al-Qurtubi*, p. 659.

[229]     *Tafsir Ibn Kathir*, Part 3, p. 38.

*Therefore, all people of the world should be called to Islam. If anyone of them refuses to do so, or refuses to pay the Jizya (head tax imposed by a Muslim state on all non-Muslims living under the protection of a Muslim government) they should be fought till they are killed.*[230]

And here is Chapter 9, Verse 123:

*O you who believe! Fight those of the disbelievers who are close to you, and let them find harshness in you; and know that Allah is with those who are Al-Muttaqun (the pious* [believers of Islamic Monotheism]*).*

In a section titled *The Order for Jihad against the Disbelievers, the Closest, then the Farthest Areas*, Ibn Kathir explained that

*Allah commands the believers to fight the disbelievers, the closest in area to the Islamic state, then the farthest. This is why the Messenger of Allah started fighting the idolators in the Arabian Peninsula. When he finished with them, and Allah gave him control over Makkah, Al-Madinah, At-Ta'if, Yemen, Yamamah, Hajr, Khaybar, Hadramawt and other Arab provinces, and the various Arab tribes entered Islam in large crowds, he then started fighting the People of the Scriptures.*[231]

---

[230]     Ibid.

[231]     *Tafsir Ibn Kathir*, Vol. 4, p. 546. Allah's commands in 9:123 were followed by Muhammad's successors:

[Muhammad was] *succeeded by Abu Bakr, through whom Allah secured Islam well. Abu Bakr prepared his Muslim army to fight the Romans, the worshippers of the crosses, and the Persians, the worshippers of Fires. He subdued Kisra (Khosrau) and Qaisar (Caisar) and their followers against their will, and spent their wealth in Allah's Way.*

106

And the modern *Tafsir Ahsanul-Bayan* pointed out:

> *The verse sets an important rule for strategy for jihad: Muslims should fight those disbelievers first who are close, followed by those who are further, then the next, and so on, in the same order. This is what the Messenger of Allah did. He fought the pagans of Arabia first...until almost all the Arab tribes embraced Islam. Then he turned to the People of the Book...Following his policy, his successors, the Rightly-Guided Caliphs, fought the Christians of the Roman Empire, and the Zoroastrians of Persia.*[232]

So we see that with 9:73 and 9:123, Allah commands Muslims to fight the non-Muslims with the intent that they become Muslims. According to many Muslim scholars, 9:73 had abrogated 2:256, and it appears that ibn Kathir believed that 9:123 had done the same.

---

> *Omar Ibn Al-Khattab...succeeded Abu Bakr, and subdued the disbelievers and pagans. He seized their kingdoms in the east and the west; safes full of wealth were brought to him, from every district, near or far...[His successor was "Othmane Ibn 'Affane"]...Islam was spread widely, and the Word of Allah was made supreme, and every time the Muslims defeated a nation, they would move on to conquer another, in response to Allah's Call: (O you who believe! Fight those among the disbelievers who are close to you.) (And let them find harshness in you.) This means that the disbelievers should find harshness when the believers have to fight them. An ideal believer is normally kind towards his fellow believer, but harsh towards his infidel enemy...*

*Tafsir Ibn Kathir*, Part 11, pp. 78-79.

[232] *Tafsir Ahsanul-Bayan*, Vol. 2, pp. 425-426.

## October 630 – Muhammad's Letter to Ibn Rubbah

While at Tabuk,[233] Muhammad wrote to the ruler and the people of Aylah demanding that they accept Islam, pay the *Jizyah*, or fight the Muslims:

> *The Apostle of Allah, my Allah bless him, wrote to Yuhannah Ibn Rubbah and (other) chiefs of the people of Aylah: You are safe. I praise Allah before you; there is no god but He. I will not fight against you unless I write to you (in advance). So, join the fold of Islam or pay the jizyah....The jizyah is a known thing. If you like that, peace might prevail over the land and sea...If you send them (my messengers) back and do not please them, I shall not accept anything from you, and shall wage war against you and make your young ones captive and shall slay your elders. Verily, I am the Apostle of Allah to communicate the truth.[234]*

Ibn Rubbah was afraid Muhammad would send a military force against him, so he went to Muhammad and agreed to pay the *Jizyah* in return for peace.[235]

## December 630 – The Thaqif Tribe Converts

The Thaqif tribe in the town of al-Ta'if realized that the Arabs around them had embraced Islam and the Thaqif did not have the military strength to resist them. As one of the Thaqif leaders noted:

> *'We are in an impasse. You have seen how the affair of this man [Muhammad] has progressed. All the Arabs*

---

233     *The Live of Muhammad (Sirat Rasul Allah)*, p. 607.

234     *Kitab al-Tabaqat al-Kabir*, Vol. 1, p. 328.

235     Ibid., p. 343.

*have accepted Islam and you lack the power to fight them,*
*so look to your case.' Thereupon Thaqif took counsel and*
*said one to another, 'Don't you see that your herds are*
*not safe; none of you can go out without being cut off.' So*
*after conferring together they decided to send a man to the*
*apostle...*[236]

A deputation of the Thaqif tribe went to Medina to meet with Muhammad. The deputation soon agreed to convert to Islam. But the deputation said that they would need time to convince the rest of the Thaqif to become Muslims and would have to lie about Muhammad to their people in order to convince them. Muhammad agreed and the deputation returned to al-Ta'if:

*The party had asked permission from the Prophet, and*
*that he be indulgent of their loose talk about him. They*
*said [to their people], "We come to you from a man who is*
*rough and rude. He takes from his affair what he wishes*

---

[236]    *The Life of Muhammad (Sirat Rasul Allah)*, p. 615. This story was similarly reported in *The History of al-Tabari: The Last Years of the Prophet*, p. 42; *Abridged Biography of Prophet Muhammad*, p. 280; and *The Life of Muhammad: Al-Waqidi's Kitab al-Maghazi*, p. 471. Shorter versions were reported in two 20th Century biographies of Muhammad:

*The Sealed Nectar*, p. 523:

> *Upon realizing that they were incapable of fighting the*
> *neighboring Arabs who had paid allegiance to the Prophet and*
> *converted to Islam, they made up their mind to dispatch a man*
> *to Allah's Messenger.*

*When the Moon Split*, p. 379:

> *...but soon the people of Ta'if realized the practical implications*
> *of holding out against the rising tide of Islam. They began to*
> *consider the problems they would face from the surrounding*
> *tribes that had embraced Islam and decided to negotiate with*
> *the Prophet.*

*and conquers with the sword. He subjugated the Bedouin and the people surrendered to him. The sons of cowards were terrified of him in their fortresses. Either he charms with his religion or frightens with the sword. He confronts us with a strong affair and terrifies us with it...we hated that he oppressed us. We think he was not fair to us. So prepare your weapons. And repair your fortress, and establish the war machines and mangonels. Take food for a year or two into your fortress. He will not besiege you for more than two years. Dig a trench behind your fortress. Hurry that, for indeed his command remains and we do not trust him.*[237]

For a day or two the people of al-Ta'if held firm to the idea of resisting Muhammad.

*Then God placed fear in their hearts and they said, "We have no power against him. He has subjugated the Bedouin, all of them. So return to him and give him what he asks and make peace with him. And write a document between you and him before he marches to us and sends his soldiers.*[238]

Ibn Kathir aptly summed up the plight of the Thaqif:

*He* [Muhammad] *would raid the land of Thaqeef and straitened them till he compelled them to enter the fold of Islam.*[239]

---

[237]    *The Life of Muhammad: Al-Waqidi's Kitab al-Maghazi*, pp. 474-475.

[238]    Ibid., p. 475. For similar reports about this see *The Sealed Nectar*, p. 524; and *When the Moon Split*, pp. 379-380.

[239]    *Winning the Hearts and Souls: Expeditions and Delegations in the Lifetime of Prophet Muhammad*, p. 154.

Ironically, there was a lot of truth in the "lie" the deputation told their people; thus the Thaqif tribe was "compelled" to become Muslims.


## March 631 - Abu Bakr Leads the Pilgrimage

During this year there were additional Koran verses "revealed" that were quite explicit in terms of how non-Muslims were to be treated and what their options were to be.

Abu Bakr, Muhammad's father-in-law and close friend, led the pilgrimage to Mecca in March 631. At this time 30-40 verses of Chapter 9 of the Koran were "revealed" and subsequently read to the non-Muslims in Mecca.[240] There is a difference of opinion about exactly which verses were "revealed," but one report stated that they consisted of the first 40 verses in Chapter 9.[241] Though there might be some disagreement about which particular verses were "revealed" and read at this time, 9:1-5 and 9:28 were definitely read to the non-Muslims in Mecca during this pilgrimage.[242] These verses were warnings to non-Muslims.

---

[240]     *Tafsir Ibn Kathir*, Vol. 4, p. 371; and *The History of al-Tabari: The Last Years of the Prophet*, pp. 78-79.

[241]     *The History of al-Tabari: The Last Years of the Prophet*, p. 77. It should be noted, however, that 9:38-40 were reported to have been "revealed" with regard to the Battle of Tabuk, which occurred earlier, in October 630; see: *Tafsir Ibn 'Abbas*, p. 234; *Tafsir Ahsanul-Bayan*, Vol. 2, pp. 354-355; *Tafsir As-Sa'di*, Vol. 2, pp. 144-145; *Tafsir Ibn Kathir*, Vol. 4, p. 427-429; *The Meaning of the Glorious Koran*, p. 191; and *The Life of Muhammad: Al-Waqidi's Kitab al-Maghazi*, p. 519.

[242]     *The Meaning of the Glorious Koran*, p. 191; *The History of al-Tabari: The Last Years of the Prophet*, pp. 78-79; *Tafsir Ibn Abbas*, pp. 228-229, and 231; *Tafsir Ahsanul-Bayan*, Vol. 2, pp. 321-326, and 342-344; *Tafsir as-Sa'di*, Vol. 2, pp. 123-126, and 136; and *The Life of Muhammad (Sirat Rasul Allah)*, pp. 618-619.

Chapter 9, Verse 1

> *Freedom from (all) obligations (is declared) from Allah and His Messenger to those of the Mushrikun (polytheists, pagans, idolaters, disbelievers in the Oneness of Allah), with whom you made a treaty.*

Chapter 9, Verse 2

> *So travel freely (O Mushrikun) for four months (as you will) throughout the land, but know that you cannot escape (from the punishment of) Allah; and Allah will disgrace the disbelievers.*

Ibn Kathir explained that these first two verses referred to

> *idolators who had indefinite treaties and those, whose treaties with Muslims ended in less than four months. The terms of these treaties were restricted to four months only. As for those whose term of peace ended at a specific date later (than the four months), then their treaties would end when their terms ended* [as long as the idolators did not break their treaty before that date]...[243]

Ibn Kathir then related the following:

> *Ibn Abu Najih quoted Mujahid: "After the announcement, the polytheists, who made treaties with the Muslims, were allowed four months, as mentioned above, then their treaty was cancelled. They made it clear to the polytheists that, unless they embraced Islam, they would wage war*

---

[243]    *Tafsir Ibn Kathir*, Vol. 4, p. 371.

*against them." As-Sudi' and Qatadah also reported the
same statement.*[244]

The *Tafsir Ahsanul-Bayan* pointed out that:

> *All of them were given permission to stay on in Mecca for
> a period of four months. It means that if they accepted
> Islam within this period, they would be allowed to stay in
> Mecca for as long as they wished, or else they would have
> to leave Mecca after four months. In case they did not
> accept any of the two courses, they would be treated as
> disbelievers at war and the Muslims would be forced to
> fight them, the purpose being to cleanse the Arabian
> Peninsula of (the darkness of) disbelief and idolatry.*[245]

The *Tafsir as-Sa'di* said that with these two verses "the enemy polytheists"
were "given a four month reprieve, during which they are protected from
the Muslims..."[246]

The *Tafsir Ibn 'Abbas* pointed out:

> *...He [Allah] will punish the disbelievers after four months
> by subjecting them to death.*[247]

This was reiterated in the *Tafsir Al-Jalalayn* when explaining 9:2:

> *'**You may travel about** safely **in the land for four months,**
> idolaters...after that you will have no security, **and know
> that you cannot thwart Allah** – escape His punishment –*

---

[244]   *Tafsir Ibn Kathir*, Part 10, p. 84.

[245]   *Tafsir Ahsanul-Bayan*, Vol. 2, pp. 322-323.

[246]   *Tafsir as-Sa'di*, Vol. 2, p. 123.

[247]   *Tafsir Ibn 'Abbas*, p. 229.

**and that Allah will humiliate the unbelievers** *in this world by killing and in the Next by the Fire.* '[248]

So 9:1 announced that the Muslims were free from all obligations to non-Muslims, and 9:2 provided a specific grace period which allowed especially the non-Muslim Meccans time to decide whether or not to become Muslims. At the end of the grace period they had to become Muslims or leave Mecca; attempting to remain in Mecca as a non-Muslim would be considered an act of war against the Muslims.

Chapter 9, Verse 3

> *And a declaration from Allah and His Messenger to mankind on the greatest day that Allah is free from (all) obligations to the Mushrikun and so is His Messenger. So if you (Mushrikun) repent, it is better for you, but if you turn away, then know that you cannot escape (from the punishment of) Allah. And give tidings (O Muhammad) of a painful torment to those who disbelieve.*

This verse was a declaration "to mankind" and repeated that Allah and Muhammad were free of all obligations to the *Mushrikun*. In this verse Allah was calling on the non-Muslims to "repent" and become Muslims. The *painful torment* for those who did not "repent" included: 1) "disgrace and affliction in this life";[249] 2) "killing and capture in this world";[250] 3) "death, exile, or captivity in this world";[251] and 4) "they will be killed after the elapse of four months."[252]

---

[248]     *Tafsir Al-Jalalayn*, p. 397.

[249]     *Tafsir Ibn Kathir*, Vol. 4, p. 373.

[250]     *Tafsir Al-Jalalayn*, p. 397.

[251]     *Tafsir as-Sa'di*, Vol. 2, p. 124.

[252]     *Tafsir Ibn 'Abbas*, p. 229.

In the next verse there was an exception for those non-Muslims who had not broken any terms of their existing treaty; for such non-Muslims, the Muslims were commanded in 9:4 to uphold the treaty until the end of its term:

Chapter 9, Verse 4

> *Except those of the Mushrikun with whom you have a treaty, and who have not subsequently failed you in aught, nor have supported anyone against you. So fulfil their treaty to them for the end of their term. Surely, Allah loves Al-Muttaqun (the pious).*

But there were also two verses "revealed" that had a direct impact on the concept of "no compulsion" found in 2:256. Those verses were 9:5 and 9:29.

## March 631 – Verses 9:5 and 9:29 Abrogate 2:256

Ibn Kathir referred to the following verse as the "Verse of the Sword":[253]

Chapter 9, Verse 5

> *Then when the Sacred Months have passed, then kill the Mushrikun wherever you find them, and capture them and besiege them, and lie in wait for them in every ambush. But if they repent [by rejecting Shirk (polytheism) and accept Islamic Monotheism] and perform As-Salat (the prayers), and give Zakat (obligatory charity), then leave their way free. Verily, Allah is Oft-Forgiving, Most Merciful.*

---

[253]     *Tafsir Ibn Kathir*, Vol. 4, pp. 375 and 377.

The Muslim scholar Yasir Qadhi made a sobering comment about this verse:

> *This was one of the last verses to be revealed, and perhaps the last verse that dealt with the treatment of the disbelievers.* [254]

So how were the disbelievers to be treated? Ibn Kathir pointed out that with this verse, the non-Muslims would "have no choice, but to die or embrace Islam."[255] Ibn Kathir also noted that the command *kill the Mushrikun wherever you find them* was a "general statement" and meant Muslims could slay them "anywhere on earth you meet them."[256]

The *Tafsir Ahsanul-Bayan* pointed out that if the *Mushrikun* became Muslims, "no action shall be taken against them."[257]

The *Tafsir as-Sa'di* explained that:

> [The non-Muslims] *are not worthy of living on this earth...because the earth is Allah's property and they are His enemies...Place all your efforts into jihad, and continuously perform jihad against them until* [they repent and become Muslims]...[Then] *Let them roam free for they are now equal to you* [Muslims]...[9:5] *is a general commandment covering all people and governing all conditions.* [258]

---

[254]    *An Introduction to the Sciences of the Qur'aan*, p. 252.

[255]    *Tafsir Ibn Kathir*, Vol. 4, p. 376.

[256]    *Tafsir Ibn Kathir*, Part 10, p. 90.

[257]    *Tafsir Ahsanul-Bayan*, Vol. 2, p. 326.

[258]    *Tafsir as-Sa'di*, Vol. 2, pp. 125-126.

Ibn Kathir aptly summed up the meaning of this verse:

> *This honorable Ayah (9:5) was called the Ayah of the*
> *Sword, about which Ad-Dahhak bin Muzahim said, "It*
> *abrogated every agreement of peace between the Prophet*
> *and any idolator, every treaty, and every term." Al-'Awfi*
> *said that Ibn 'Abbas commented: "No idolator had any*
> *more treaty or promise of safety ever since Surah Bara'ah*
> *[Chapter 9] was revealed. The four months, in addition to,*
> *all peace treaties conducted before Bara'ah was revealed*
> *and announced had ended by the tenth of the month of*
> *Rabi' Al-Akhir [July 16, 631].* "[259]

So, according to ibn 'Abbas, the four month grace period mentioned in 9:2, and all existing peace treaties between Muslims and non-Muslims prior to the "revelation" of Chapter 9, had ended by July 16, 631.

As mentioned previously, some Muslim scholars believed that 2:256 had been abrogated by 9:73, which had been "revealed" a few months earlier. Now, with 9:5 we have another verse in Chapter 9 abrogating 2:256.

But the Muslim scholar As-Suddi said there was an additional verse that had abrogated 2:256; that verse was 9:29.[260] This verse was the first command from Allah to the Muslims to specifically fight the Jews and Christians.[261]

---

[259]    *Tafsir Ibn Kathir*, Vol. 4, p. 377.

[260]    As mentioned previously, the Muslim scholar as-Suddi said that 2:256 was abrogated when Muhammad was commanded to fight the People of the Book (Jews and Christians) in Chapter 9 of the Koran (that command is found in 9:29); see *Al-Wahidi's Asbab al-Nuzul*, p. 37; and *Tafsir Al-Qurtubi*, p. 661.

[261]    *Tafsir Ibn Kathir*, Part 10, p. 119.

9:29 was "revealed" as a result of the anticipated negative commercial impact on the Meccans from the "revelation" of 9:28, which had also been read to the non-Muslims in Mecca; here is 9:28:

> O you who believe (in Allah's Oneness and in His Messenger Muhammad)! Verily, the Mushrikun are Najasun (impure). So let them not come near Al-Masjid Al-Haram (at Makkah) after this year; and if you fear poverty, Allah will enrich you if He wills, out of His bounty. Surely, Allah is All-Knowing, All-Wise.

This verse told the non-Muslims that after this year they would no longer be permitted to come into Mecca because of their impurity.

But after 9:28 was "revealed" there was concern among the Meccans that they would lose money if the non-Muslims were prohibited from coming to Mecca:

> ...when Allah commanded that the polytheists be prevented from coming near Masjid Al-Haram whether during the Hajj or any other time, the Quraish said: "It will certainly infringe on our commerce and markets during Hajj, and it will deprive us from our gains," but Allah compensated them for that with the command to wage war on the People of the Book until they become Muslims or they pay the Jizyah with willful submission, and feel themselves subdued. [262]

---

[262]     *Winning the Hearts and Souls: Expeditions and Delegations in the Lifetime of Prophet Muhammad*, p. 116. The same explanation for the "revelation" of 9:29 was given in *Tafsir Ibn Kathir*, Vol. 4, pp. 403-404; and *The Life of Muhammad (Sirat Rasul Allah)*, p. 620.

And there were additional sources of "commerce" available after the expulsion of the polytheists:

> A series of Muslim conquests followed and a wealth of spoils of war came to the Muslims. Moreover, when the whole of the

Here is 9:29, *the command to wage war on the People of the Book*:

> *Fight against those who believe not in Allah, nor in the*
> *Last Day, nor forbid that which has been forbidden by*
> *Allah and His Messenger (Muhammad), and those who*
> *acknowledge not the religion of truth (i.e. Islam) among*
> *the people of the Scripture (Jews and Christians), until*
> *they pay the Jizyah with willing submission, and feel*
> *themselves subdued.*

So instead of being presented with just the choice of either converting to Islam or fighting to the death, as commanded in 9:5, Jews and Christians were given an additional option: they could *pay the Jizyah with willing submission, and feel themselves subdued.* And with 9:29 we have another verse that abrogated 2:256.

Also "revealed" during this time period was 9:33:

> *It is He Who has sent His Messenger (Muhammad) with*
> *guidance and the religion of truth (Islam), to make it*
> *superior over all religions even though the Mushrikun*
> *(polytheists, pagans, idolaters, disbelievers in the Oneness*
> *of Allah) hate (it).*

In a section titled *Islam is the Religion That will dominate over all Other Religions*, Ibn Kathir used the words of Muhammad to explain this verse:

> *Imam Ahmad recorded from Tamim Ad-Dari that he said,*
> *I heard the Messenger of Allah saying, "This matter*
> *(Islam) will keep spreading as far as the night and day*

---

> *Arabian Peninsula had been converted to Islam, there was an*
> *influx of pilgrims, their numbers increased...*

*Tafsir Ahsanul-Bayan*, Vol. 2, p. 345. The *Tafsir Al-Jalalayn* (p. 404) also mentioned Allah would enrich the Muslims "through conquest and *jizya*" to replace the lost commerce with the polytheists.

119

*reach, until Allah will not leave a house made of mud or hair, but will make this religion enter it, while bringing might to a mighty person (a Muslim) and humiliation to a disgraced person (who rejects Islam). Might with which Allah elevates Islam (and its people) and disgrace with which Allah humiliates disbelief (and its people). "[263]*

Ibn Kathir then added,

*Tamim Ad-Dari [who was a Christian before Islam] used to say, "I have come to know the meaning of this Hadith in my own people. Those who became Muslims among them acquired goodness, honor and might. Disgrace, humiliation and Jizyah befell those who remained disbelievers. "[264]*

## Chapter 49 of the Koran – Obey Muhammad

Chapter 49 of the Koran was "revealed" during this year.[265] Here again we have repeated admonitions for the Muslims to obey Allah and to obey Muhammad:

Chapter 49, Verse 1

*O you who believe! Make not (a decision) in advance before Allah and His Messenger, and fear Allah. Verily, Allah is All-Hearing, All-Knowing.*

---

[263]     *Tafsir Ibn Kathir*, Vol. 4, pp. 412-413.

[264]     Ibid., p. 413.

[265]     *The Meaning of the Glorious Koran*, p. 533.

Ibn Kathir explained that this verse meant Muslims were not to "rush in making decisions" before Muhammad had done so; rather, they were to "follow his lead in all matters."[266]

The *Tafsir Ahsanul-Bayan* pointed out:

> *Allah forbids believers to decide on their own on a matter relating to religion or give precedence to their own opinions but obey Allah and His messenger.*[267]

And with 49:15 we find that the true believers are only those who believe in Allah and Muhammad:

> *Only those are the believers who have believed in Allah and His Messenger...*

---

[266]     *Tafsir Ibn Kathir*, Vol. 9, p. 184.

[267]     *Tafsir Ahsanul-Bayan*, Vol. 5, pp. 200-201.

# Forced Conversions Continue

*Jabir said: "We were commanded to strike with the sword whoever opposes the Book of Allah."*[268]

Even after the *Year of the Deputations* ended, Muhammad continued to send out Muslim military forces to "invite" non-Muslim tribes to Islam.

## June 631 – An "Invitation" to the Banu 'Abd al-Madan

Muhammad sent Khalid with a Muslim force to the Banu 'Abd al-Madan.

> *Khalid was instructed to invite them to accept Islam for three days, and if they refused, he was allowed to use force to make them subjects of the Islamic state.*[269]

The Banu 'Abd al-Madan accepted Islam.

## July 631 – An "Invitation" to the Banu al-Harith b. Ka'b

Muhammad sent Khalid bin al-Walid with a force of 400 Muslims. Khalid was ordered to spend three days inviting the Banu al-Harith b. Ka'b to

---

[268]    *Tafsir Ibn Kathir*, Vol. 7, p. 496.

> *Book of Allah means both the Qur'an and Hadith because both of* [sic] *are from Allah.*

*Sunan Ibn Majah*, Vol. 3, Comment to *Hadith* No. 2549, p. 462.

[269]    *When the Moon Split*, p. 384.

Islam. If they accepted, he was to stay with them and teach them about Islam. If they declined, he was to fight them. The Banu al-Harith b. Ka'b accepted Islam.[270]

## December 631 – An "Invitation" to the Madhhij

Muhammad sent a Muslim army of 300 warriors under the command of 'Ali bin Abi Talib to the land of the Madhhij in Yemen. Muhammad told 'Ali:

> *When you alight in their courtyard, do not fight them until they fight you; if they attack you, do not fight them until they kill one of you. If they kill one of you, do not fight them or blame them, but show them patience. Say to them, 'Will you say that there is but one God?' And if they say, "Yes,' say, 'Will you pray?' And if they say 'Yes,' say, 'Will you take from your property and give charity to your poor?' And if they say 'Yes,' do not desire anything else.*[271]

Muhammad commanded a peaceful approach, but 'Ali acted differently:

> *He set out with three hundred riders, and their cavalry was the first to enter that land. When he reached near the land that he desired – which was the land of Madhhij – he dispersed his companions, and they brought plunder and prisoners and women and children and cattle and sheep and other things, by force...Then he met a group and*

---

[270]    *Winning the Hearts and Souls: Expeditions and Delegations in the Lifetime of Prophet Muhammad*, pp. 231-233; *The Life of Muhammad (Sirat Rasul Allah)*, p. 645; *The History of al-Tabari: The Last Years of the Prophet*, pp. 82-83; and *Kitab al-Tabaqat al-Kabir*, Vol. 1, p. 399 (Ibn Sa'd reported that Khalid was ordered to invite the Banu al-Harith b. Ka'b to Islam three <u>times</u> before he fought them).

[271]    *The Life of Muhammad: Al-Waqidi's Kitab al-Maghazi*, p. 528.

*invited them to Islam and enticed them with it* [the plunder]. *But they refused and aimed at his companions...Then 'Ali attacked them with his companions and killed twenty of their men, and they dispersed defeated... 'Ali refrained from seeking them out; he invited them to Islam, and they hastened and responded. A group of their leaders approached and granted allegiance to Islam.*[272]

'Ali later wrote to Muhammad explaining

*that he met a group from Zabid,*[273] *and others, and that he invited them to Islam and informed them that if they converted he would refrain from them. But they refused that and so he fought them. 'Ali said: And God provided me with victory over them, until some of them were killed. Then, they responded to what was offered them and they entered Islam...*[274]

Ibn Sa'd provided another report of what happened when 'Ali met the Madhhij force:

['Ali] *invited them to embrace Islam. They refused and threw arrows and stones...Then 'Ali with his companions, led an attack against them and killed twenty men. They were dispersed and fled away. He restrained from pursuing them but he invited them to embrace Islam. They promptly responded; and a party of their chiefs took oath* [sic] *of allegiance...*[275]

---

272    Ibid.

273    A town in Western Yemen.

274    *The Life of Muhammad: Al-Waqidi's Kitab al-Maghazi*, p. 529.

275    *Kitab al-Tabaqat al-Kabir*, Vol. 2, p. 210.

Even though 'Ali went against Muhammad's original command, there was no report that Muhammad was displeased with 'Ali's actions. A likely explanation for this is to be found in Muhammad's reaction when four Muslims complained to him about 'Ali's conduct toward a female slave in another expedition. Muhammad became angry and said to them:

> *"What do you want from 'Ali?! Indeed 'Ali is from me, and I am from him, and he is the ally of every believer after me."*[276]

The modern commentary for this *hadith* explained that the phrase *'Ali is from me and I am from him* meant not only the family connection, but it was "also to emphasize" that Ali's "conduct and character resembles" that of Muhammad.[277]

## December 631 – An "Invitation" to Jurash

Surad b. 'Abdallah al-Azdi led a delegation from the al-Azd tribe to Medina and they converted to Islam. Muhammad then appointed Surad to lead a Muslim army

> *to wage war against the polytheists of the tribe of Yaman...He set out and alighted at Jurash which was a strongly fortified city and where the tribes of Yaman had taken shelter. He (Surad) invited them to embrace Islam but they declined. He besieged them for a month...Then he retreated to a mountain...They thought that he had fled, and came out to pursue him. He arrayed his forces, and attacked them. Muslims put them to the sword as they liked.*[278]

---

[276]     *Jami' At-Tirmidhi*, Vol. 6, No. 3712, pp. 386-387.

[277]     Ibid., p. 387.

[278]     *Kitab al-Tabaqat al-Kabir*, Vol. 1, pp. 397-398.

Surad's Muslim army inflicted heavy losses on the people of Jurash, and they soon embraced Islam.

## February 632 - Muhammad's Farewell Pilgrimage

About four months before he died Muhammad took his final pilgrimage to Mecca and explicitly stated that he had been commanded to fight people until they became Muslims. During his speech on the day after the sacrificial animals were slaughtered, Muhammad said,

> *Indeed I was commanded to fight people until they say there is but one God, and when they say it, their blood and their property is protected and they are answerable to God.*[279]

In another speech during this pilgrimage he repeated the importance of following his example and teachings:

---

[279]     *The Life of Muhammad: Al-Waqidi's Kitab al-Maghazi*, p. 544. There are numerous *hadiths* from various narrators that Muhammad said he had been commanded to fight people until they accepted Islam, e.g.:

> *It has been narrated on the authority of 'Abdullah b. Umar that the Messenger of Allah said: I have been commanded to fight against people till they testify that there is no god but Allah, and Muhammad is the Messenger of Allah, they establish the prayer, and pay the Zakat. If they do it, their blood and property are guaranteed protection on my behalf except when justified by law, and their affairs rest with Allah.*

*Sahih Muslim*, Vol. 1, No. 22, pp. 21-22. There was no time frame indicated for Muhammad's statement in this *hadith*, or in other similar *hadiths*, e.g.: *Sahih Al-Bukhari*, Vol. 1, Book 2, No. 25, p. 66; Vol. 4, Book 56, No. 2946, p. 126; *Jami' At-Tirmidhi*, Vol. 5, No. 2606, p. 15, and No. 2608, pp. 17-18; Vol. 6, No. 3341, p. 76; *Sunan Ibn Majah*, Vol. 1, Nos. 71-72, pp. 123-124; *Sunan An-Nasa'i*, Vol. 4, No. 3092, p. 18, and No. 3097, pp. 21-22; and *Sunan Abu Dawud*, Vol. 3, No. 2641, p. 277.

*I have conveyed the Message, and have left you with
something which, if you hold fast to it, you will never go
astray: that is, the Book of God and the sunnah of His
Prophet.*[280]

So in February 632 Muhammad specifically stated that he had been
commanded to fight people until they became Muslims, and Muslims were
to follow his example.


## May 632 – Kill Him Who Disobeys Allah

Muhammad ordered Usama ibn Zayd ibn Harithah to attack the Byzantines
at Ubna (this was the second Expedition to Mu'ta).  Muhammad said:

*Fight in the name of Allah, in the way of Allah, and kill
him who disobeys Allah.*[281]

Those who disobey Allah are non-Muslims, so Muhammad had
commanded Usama to fight and kill the non-Muslims simply because they
were not Muslims.

Muhammad's death on June 7th delayed the attack.  Soon afterward, when
Usama led his force to Ubna, he said,

---

[280]     *The History of al-Tabari: The Last Years of the Prophet*, p. 113.  Ibn
Ishaq reported this statement with slightly different wording:

*I have left with you something which if you will hold fast to it
you will never fall into error – a plain indication, the book of
God and the practice of His prophet, so give good heed to what
I say.*

*The Life of Muhammad (Sirat Rasul Allah)*, p. 651.

[281]     *Kitab al-Tabaqat al-Kabir*, Vol. 2, p. 235.

*But the Messenger of God commanded me and this was his last command to me: To hasten the march and to be ahead of the news. And to raid them, without inviting them [to Islam], and to destroy and burn.*[282]

## June 7, 632 – The Death of Muhammad

A few days before he died, Muhammad said

*I leave with you two things. As long as you hold them tightly, you will never go astray: they are the Book of Allah and my Sunnah.*[283]

On the day he died, Muhammad said,

*I only declare lawful what Allah has declared lawful in His Book and I do not declare anything unlawful but what Allah has declared unlawful in His Book.*[284]

On that day Muhammad also said:

*It has been narrated by 'Umar b. Al-Khattab that he heard the Messenger of Allah (may peace be upon him) saying: I*

---

[282] *The Life of Muhammad: Al-Waqidi's Kitab al-Maghazi*, p. 549.

[283] *When the Moon Split*, p. 403.

[284] *Kitab al-Tabaqat al-Kabir*, Vol. 2, p. 268. It was also reported that Muhammad simply said:

*O people! do* [sic] *not hold me responsible for anything. I only declare lawful what Allah made lawful and declare unlawful what Allah made unlawful.*

Ibid., p. 319.

*will expel the Jews and Christians from the Arabian Peninsula and will not leave any but Muslims.*[285]

And another narrator reported similar words of Muhammad:

*Yahya related to me from Malik from Isma'il ibn Abi Hakim that he heard 'Umar ibn 'Abd al-'Aziz say, "One of the last things that the Messenger of Allah, may Allah bless him and grant him peace, said was, 'May Allah fight the Jews and the Christians! They took the graves of their Prophets as places of prostration. Two deens [religions] shall not co-exist in the land of the Arabs.'"*[286]

---

[285]    *Sahih Muslim*, Vol. 5, No. 1767, p. 189. Versions of this *hadith*, also specifically mentioning Jews and Christians, are in *Sunan Abu Dawud*, Vol. 3, No. 3030, p. 517; *Jami' At-Tirmidhi*, Vol. 3, Nos. 1606-1607, p. 368; *Musnad Imam Ahmad Bin Hanbal*, Vol. 1, No. 201, p. 128; and *The Sealed Nectar*, p. 554 (where it is stated that Muhammad said this four days before his death). For reports that Muhammad actually mentioned expelling non-Muslims in general, see *Sahih Al-Bukhari*, Vol. 4, Book 56, No. 3053, pp. 179-180; and Vol. 5, Book 64, No. 4431, pp. 438-439; *The Life of Muhammad (Sirat Rasul Allah)*, p. 689; and *The History of al-Tabari: The Last Years of the Prophet*, p. 175.

[286]    Malik ibn Anas ibn Malik ibn Abi 'Amir al-Asbahi, *Al-Muwatta of Imam Malik ibn Anas: The First Formulation of Islamic Law*, trans. Aisha Abdurrahman Bewley (Inverness, Scotland: Madinah Press, 2004), 45.5.17.

# Conclusion

The Religion of Islam began in Mecca in the year 610. Over the next 12 years two fundamental doctrines were established:

1.  Muslims were to obey Allah, and specifically obey Muhammad.

2.  Muhammad spoke for Allah, commanded what was made permissible by Allah, and forbade what was forbidden by Allah.

And in those early years there was a militant component to Islam being introduced:

1.  Those who converted to Islam would rule over and be in a state of hostility toward non-Muslims;

2.  The non-Muslims would have to submit to Allah and Islam, willingly or unwillingly;

3.  And there was the threat of "slaughter" for those who refused to become Muslims.

These aspects of early Islam accompanied the Muslims as they emigrated to Medina in the Summer and Fall of 622.

We then saw that over the subsequent three years: 1) 4:47 threatened Jews and Christians if they did not believe in Islam; 2) the "Command for Jihad" in 2:216 was "revealed," commanding Muslims to fight non-Muslims for the Cause of Allah; 3) according to 8:39 that fighting was to continue until Islam was the only religion, because, according to 3:85,

Islam was the only religion acceptable to Allah; and 4) in 3:83 Muslims were told that all creatures would submit to Allah, willingly or unwillingly.

So during the first 15 years of Islam the militant component was developing as a result of Koran verses proclaiming the supremacy of Islam, intolerance and threats toward non-Muslims, and the command to fight non-Muslims until Islam was supreme. This component was to be put into action by other verses commanding Muslims to follow both Allah and Muhammad.

And in those early years Muhammad himself was already talking about Muslim military conquests and the subjugation and slaughtering of non-Muslims. The development of this theme continued through the successful Muslim siege of the Banu Qaynuqa toward the end of this time period. And as we saw, Muhammad had initially wanted to kill the captive Jews of Banu Qaynuqa after they had refused the "invitation" to Islam, but he relented and expelled them instead.

However, in November 624, only seven months later, an "invitation" to Islam included only two options for the individual recipient: in front of Muhammad a captive was given the stark choice of either converting to Islam or being killed. The captive converted to Islam and was spared by Muhammad.

But this was supposed to have changed in August 625 with the "revelation" of 2:256, in which Allah stated there was to be "no compulsion in religion"; after the "revelation" of this verse there should not have been any more thoughts of forced conversions to Islam.

But as we saw, a little over two years after that "revelation" numerous incidents started occurring in which Muhammad, or Muslims acting under his authority, gave non-Muslims the option of converting to Islam, fighting to the death, or at times, paying the *Jizyah*.

Was Muhammad actually making permissible what he knew Allah had made impermissible? The short answer is "No." As Qadi 'Iyad wrote:

131

*It is not possible for the Prophet to contradict any of the Shari'a that he conveyed and communicated from his Lord or any of what was revealed to him by Allah as revelation, either intentionally or unintentionally, whether in a state of pleasure or anger, or in health or sickness.*[287]

And as we saw earlier, Muhammad said,

*"Why do some people refrain from doing something which I do? By Allah, I know Allah more than they, and I am more submissive to Him than they."*[288]

If Muhammad was submissive to and could not contradict Allah, then something happened to the doctrinal authority of 2:256.

## Takhsees

One might think that Muhammad's actions could be examples of *takhsees*, because, as we saw previously, *takhsees* allows the *Sunnah* to limit or restrict a verse of the Koran.

However, 2:256 makes a timeless, blanket statement that there are to be no forced conversions in Islam; Muhammad appeared to be going against that by giving non-Muslims the option of converting to Islam, being killed, or paying the *Jizyah*.

So there is no limitation or restriction involved here. Muhammad's actions did not limit, but rather directly contradicted 2:256. So let's consider the Doctrine of Abrogation.

---

[287]    *Muhammad, Messenger of Allah: Ash-Shifa of Qadi 'Iyad*, p. 300.

[288]    *Sahih Al-Bukhari*, Vol. 9, Book 96, No. 7301, p. 246.

## The *Sunnah* Abrogating the Koran

As we saw when looking at the Doctrine of Abrogation, authoritative
Muslim scholars, including the founders of three of the four major Sunni
Schools of Sharia Law, believed that the *Sunnah* alone could, under certain
circumstances, abrogate the Koran. This was because both the Koran and
the *Sunnah* were "forms of revelation from Allah" and could therefore
abrogate one another.

The criterion for this kind of abrogation was that the abrogating *hadith*
from the *Sunnah* had to be "authentic" or "*mutawaatir.*" As noted earlier,
this meant the *hadith* had to have "been reported by many narrators and
with different chains of transmission."

Let's take a similar approach with the reports we have relied on in this
book from those who are considered to be authoritative Muslim
scholars.[289] And as we can see in the list below, these Muslim scholars
lived from the 8th through the 21st Centuries:

> *The Life of Muhammad (Sirat Rasul Allah)* – Muhammad ibn Ishaq (704-
> 768)

---

[289]    For example, works of the following scholars we have used are
considered to be among "the traditional Sunni Islamic Canon":

1.   Commentaries by al-Qurtubi, Jalalayn, ibn Kathir, and al-Wahidi's
     *Asbab al Nuzul*;

2.   The *hadith* collections of al-Bukhari, Muslim, an-Nasa'i, at-Tirmidhi,
     Abu Dawud (al-Sijistani), and ibn Majah; and ibn Hanbal's *Musnad*;

3.   The traditional biographical and historical works of *Sira* by ibn Ishaq, ibn
     Sa'd, al-Waqidi, and al-Tabari, and the *Muwatta'* of Imam Malik.

*The Muslim 500 – The World's 500 Most Influential Muslims 2016*, The Royal
Islamic Strategic Studies Centre (Amman, Jordan), p. 24. This report and the
reports from previous years are available at http://themuslim500.com/.

*Al-Muwatta of Imam Malik ibn Anas: The First Formulation of Islamic Law*, Malik ibn Anas ibn Malik ibn Abi 'Amir al-Asbahi (c. 711-795)

*The Expeditions (Kitab al-Maghazi)* - Ma'mar ibn Rashid (714-770)

*The Life of Muhammad: Al-Waqidi's Kitab al-Maghazi* - Muhammad b. 'Umar al-Waqidi (747-823)

*Musnad Imam Ahmad Bin Hanbal*, Ahmad bin Muhammad bin Hanbal ash-Shaibani (780-855)

*Kitab al-Tabaqat al-Kabir* – Abu 'Abd Allah Muhammad ibn Sa'd ibn Mani' al-Zuhri al-Basri (784-845)

*The Origins of the Islamic State* - Ahmad ibn Yahya ibn Jabir al-Baladhuri (d. 892)

*The History of al-Tabari* - Abu Ja'far Muhammad b. Jarir al-Tabari (839-923)

The "Six Books of *Hadith*": Al-Bukhari (810-870), Muslim (821-875), Abu Dawud (824-897), At-Tirmidhi (827-901), ibn Majah (831-895), and An-Nasa'i (836-925).

*Tafsir Ibn Abbas* (circa 900)

*Al-Wahidi's Asbab al-Nuzul* - Abu'l-Hasan 'Ali ibn Ahmad ibn Muhammad ibn 'Ali al-Wahidi (d. 1075)

*Tafsir Al-Qurtubi*, Abu 'Abdullah Muhammad ibn Ahmad al-Ansari al-Qurtubi (1214-1273)

*In Defence of the True Faith / Winning the Hearts and Souls / Tafsir Ibn Kathir* - 'Imaduddeen Isma'eel ibn Katheer (ibn Kathir) al-Qurashi (1323-1396)

*Tafsir Al-Jalalayn* - Jalalu'd-Din al-Mahalli (1389-1459) and Jalalu'd-Din as-Suyuti (1445-1505)

*Abridged Biography of Prophet Muhammad* - Muhammad ibn 'Abdul Wahhab at-Tamimi (1703-1791)

*Tafsir As-Sa'di* - 'Abd ar-Rahman b. Nasir as-Sa'di (1885-1956)

*The Sealed Nectar / When the Moon Split* – Safiur-Rahman al-Mubarakpuri (1942-2006)

*Tafsir Ahsanul-Bayan* - Salahuddin Yusuf (20th Century-Present)

We saw reports in the writings of many of these authoritative Muslim scholars that even after the "revelation" of 2:256 there were numerous incidents in which Muhammad, or his Muslim warriors, gave non-Muslims the option of converting to Islam, fighting to the death, or, at times, paying the *Jizyah*. And many of these incidents had been reported by more than one of these Muslim scholars over the course of about 1,300 years.

Would authoritative Muslim scholars really have followed each other in creating or repeating lies about Muhammad for over a thousand years? That would be blasphemy. And giving credence to such a claim would require us to dismiss as blasphemous fiction works that for centuries have provided extensive knowledge about Muhammad and Islam. Such an action would leave a gaping hole in that knowledge and could perhaps raise questions about the credibility of other Muslim scholars.

But these Muslim scholars have been considered authoritative and have been relied on for many centuries, meaning that their reports of forced conversions to Islam during the life of Muhammad have been similarly accepted.

Let's then consider the actual English translations of those works. Most are translations done by Muslims and published by Muslim publishing houses. Would these Muslim translators and Muslim publishing houses really be partners in reporting lies about Muhammad?

And consider especially *The Life of Muhammad (Sirat Rasul Allah)*. The translation that we used was published by Oxford University Press, and printed in 2007 by Mas Printers, both located in Karachi, Pakistan. In Pakistan there are blasphemy laws that make it a crime to criticize Islam. In 1986, Clause 295-C was added to the law to specifically punish blasphemy against Muhammad; the penalty was death or life in prison. In

1991, the option of life in prison was removed and the only penalty left was death.[290] Taking this into consideration, it would be difficult to claim that in Pakistan the Oxford University Press published, and Mas Printers printed, a book that reported lies about Muhammad.

So we can either dismiss our authoritative Muslim scholars as merely writers of blasphemous fiction, and assert that our Muslim translators and publishers have joined in with that blasphemy, or we can accept that these reports about Muhammad ordering forced conversions to Islam are accurate and, consequently, provide us the evidence to show that the *Sunnah* of Muhammad had abrogated 2:256, starting in December 627. The evidence supports the second choice.

However, along this line, there is a possibility that 2:256 had actually been abrogated only two months after it was "revealed" by Muhammad's actions at the Expedition of Dhat al-Riqa in October 625. Considering the impact his Muslim army had, with one of the results being that many of the Bedouins felt the subsequent necessity to convert to Islam, it is possible that this incident was actually an example of 2:256 being abrogated by Muhammad's use of force. If this was the case, then 2:256 had doctrinal authority for no more than two months. However, due to the lack of more detailed information about Muhammad's statements and the actual actions of the Muslims, there is not enough evidence at this time to definitively support such a conclusion.

Nevertheless, in February 632 Muhammad confirmed that 2:256 had been abrogated by his *Sunnah* when he said:

> *Indeed I was commanded to fight people until they say there is but one God, and when they say it, their blood and their property is protected and they are answerable to God.*[291]

---

[290]     *Pakistan Blasphemy Laws, Ending the Abuse of the Blasphemy Laws*, at http://www.pakistanblasphemylaw.com/?page_id=15.

[291]     *The Life of Muhammad: Al-Waqidi's Kitab al-Maghazi*, p. 544.

## The Koran Abrogating the Koran

But the Koran itself also abrogated 2:256. As noted earlier, according to various authoritative Muslim scholars 2:256 was abrogated at different times by these five Koran verses:

1.  48:16 (March 628)

2.  9:73 and 9:123 (October 630)

3.  9:5 and 9:29 (March 631)

To this list of abrogating verses I would add 2:193, which was "revealed" in March 629.

So Muhammad's actions after March 628 were supported by 48:16 abrogating 2:256 and the subsequent abrogations of 2:256 by other Koran verses.

But 48:16 was "revealed" about three months after the incident at Dumat al-Jandal, so at the time of that incident 2:256 had not yet been abrogated by 48:16. And, for the sake of argument, what if some would claim that the six verses above had not really abrogated 2:256, and that the *Sunnah* could not abrogate the Koran? What then about the December 627 expedition to Dumat al-Jandal and subsequent incidents in which non-Muslims were given the choice of converting to Islam, fighting, or paying the *Jizyah*? Was Muhammad really making permissible what he knew Allah had made impermissible?

The answer is "No," because starting in the early Meccan days, Allah told the Muslims that Muhammad spoke only that which Allah commanded him, and Allah commanded the Muslims to obey Muhammad. Similar commands from Allah continued up to the "revelation" of 2:256. And after the "revelation" of 2:256, and prior to the expedition to Dumat al-Jandal, Allah again repeatedly told the Muslims to obey Muhammad and forbade them from disagreeing with Muhammad.

One such command was found in 59:7, and it is important because it was "revealed" shortly after 2:256. So, whenever there was an irreconcilable conflict between those two verses in particular, the command to obey Muhammad found in 59:7 abrogated the message of "no compulsion" found in 2:256. And 59:7 was a general command to the Muslims to obey Muhammad in all his commands and prohibitions. As we saw, the "revelation" of 59:7 also provided a specific Koranic basis for Muslims to equate what Muhammad said with the commands of Allah in the Koran.

The following *hadith* provides us an example of how well ingrained this idea became with the Muslims:

> *Al-Miswar bin Yazid Al-Maliki narrated that the Messenger of Allah once recited in the prayer, and left out something without reciting it. So a person said to him (after the prayer): "O Messenger of Allah! You left out such and such a Verse!" The Messenger of Allah said: "Then why did you not remind me of it?" In his narration Sulaiman (one of the narrators) added (that the man responded): "I presumed that it had been abrogated."[292]*

The belief that Muhammad spoke for Allah and that his words were equated with the Koran was reinforced by another incident that occurred during the time period before, or several months after, the expedition to Dumat al-Jandal. This incident involved the changing of the Islamic penalty for adultery.

A verse of the Koran addressing the penalty for adultery was "revealed" during the time period of June 625 – June 626 (4 AH):

Chapter 4, Verse 15:

> *And those of your women who commit illegal sexual intercourse, take the evidence of four witnesses from*

---

[292]    *Sunan Abu Dawud*, Vol. 1, No. 907, p. 531.

*amongst you against them; and if they testify, confine them (i.e. women) to houses until death comes to them or Allah ordains for them some (other) way.*

So the focus of this verse was on how to punish women who had committed "illegal sexual intercourse." But this verse left an opening for something to come later with this ending statement: *or Allah ordains for them some (other) way.* It was this ending statement that resulted in the following *hadith*: [293]

> *'Ubada b. As-Samit reported: Allah's Messenger (SAW) saying: Receive (teaching) from me, receive (teaching) from me. Allah has ordained a way for those (women). When an unmarried male commits adultery with an unmarried female (they should receive) one hundred lashes and banishment for one year. And in case of married male committing adultery with a married female, they shall receive one hundred lashes and be stoned to death.*[294]

The *hadith* about this *other way* occurred about a year or two after the "revelation" of 4:15.[295] And as we saw previously, during that same time period there were many Koran verses being "revealed" that commanded Muslims to obey Muhammad. So even though there was no Koran verse specifically commanding the stoning of adulterers,[296] the fact that this

---

[293]     *Tafsir Al-Jalalayn*, p. 180; *Tafsir Ibn Kathir*, Vol. 2, pp. 400-401; and *Tafsir Ahsanul-Bayan*, Vol. 1, p. 430.

[294]     *Sahih Muslim*, Vol. 5, No. 1690, p. 131. *SAW* is the abbreviation for *Sallallahu 'Alaihe wa Sallam*. This is translated as, "May the peace and blessings of Allah be upon him."

[295]     Ibid., n. 1, p. 141, in which the time frame for this *hadith* was circa 5 AH to 6 AH, covering the time period of June 626 – May 628.

[296]     It should be noted that there was a claim that a "stoning" verse had actually been "revealed," but it had not been included in the compilation of the

command came from Muhammad, who spoke for Allah, made it as valid for the Muslims as if there had been an actual "stoning" verse in the Koran. As ibn 'Abbas said,

> *He who disbelieves in stoning (the adulterer to death) will have inadvertently disbelieved in the Qur'an...*[297]

So according to ibn 'Abbas, Muhammad's command about stoning adulterers had the same authority as if there had been such a verse in the Koran.

We can see that both 59:7 and the changing of the penalty for adultery provided a Koranic basis for giving Muhammad the authority to abrogate 2:256. So the actions and teachings of Muhammad, under the guidance of Allah and given doctrinal authority and Koranic equivalence by numerous verses in the Koran, legitimized forced conversions to Islam. Through the actions of Muhammad, the Koran had abrogated the Koran.

The command of "no compulsion" in Islam was a unique command that had doctrinal authority for only a little over two years. It was abrogated both by the *Sunnah* and by the Koran. Its short lifetime was preceded and followed by commands that non-Muslims were to be given the option of converting to Islam, fighting to the death, or, at times, paying the *Jizyah*. Muhammad was indeed the militant prophet of a militant religion that supported forced conversions to Islam.

As Sulaiman b. Buraid reported:

> *...when the Messenger of Allah (may peace be upon him) appointed anyone as leader of an army or detachment he*

---

Koran after Muhammad's death. For more information about this see "The Significance of Muhammad" in Stephen M. Kirby, *Letting Islam Be Islam: Separating Truth From Myth* (Charleston, South Carolina: CreateSpace, 2012), pp. 60-62.

[297]     *Tafsir Ibn Kathir*, Vol. 3, pp. 131-132.

*would especially exhort him to fear Allah and to be good
to the Muslims who were with him. He would say: Fight
in the name of Allah and in the way of Allah. Fight
against those who disbelieve in Allah. Make a holy
war...When you meet your enemies who are polytheists,
invite them to three courses of action...Invite them to
(accept) Islam; if they respond to you, accept it from them
and desist from fighting against them...If they refuse to
accept Islam, demand from them the Jizya. If they agree
to pay, accept it from them and hold off your hands. If
they refuse to pay the tax, seek Allah's help and fight
them...*[298]

*Indeed in the Messenger of Allah (Muhammad) you have a good
example to follow for him who hopes for (the Meeting with) Allah
and the Last Day, and remembers Allah much.* (33:21)

---

[298]     *Sahih Muslim*, Vol. 5, No. 1731R1, pp. 162-163. This *hadith* about
Muhammad ordering these three courses of action was also reported in *Sunan Abu
Dawud*, Vol. 3, No. 2612, pp. 262-264; *Sunan Ibn Majah*, Vol. 4, No. 2858, pp.
98-100; and *Jami' At-Tirmidhi*, Vol. 3, No. 1617, pp. 376-378.

As ibn 'Abbas plainly stated:

*It was narrated that Ibn 'Abbas said: The Messenger of Allah
did not fight any people until he called them [to Islam first].*

*Musnad Imam Ahmad Bin Hanbal*, Vol. 2, No. 2053, p. 305.

# Appendix 1: Don't Question Muhammad

*Obeying the Messenger is part of obeying Allah since Allah commands that he be obeyed. True obedience is obedience to Allah's command and therefore obedience to His Prophet.*[299]

Muslims were openly discouraged from asking Muhammad too many questions. As we saw in the chapter on the Doctrine of Abrogation, the short-lived 58:12 was "revealed" in order to place some limits on the number of people seeking private discussions with Muhammad. And later, 5:101 was "revealed" expressing Allah's disapproval of the unnecessary questioning of Muhammad.

To further limit questions, Muhammad said that Allah had intentionally

*left some things without rulings...so do not ask about them.*[300]

Muhammad also explicitly said not to ask him about things he had left out:

*Quoting Ibn Abbas, Al-Awfi said: "The Prophet announced to people, saying: "O people! Pilgrimage has been prescribed for you." A man from Banu Asad clan asked: 'O Allah's Messenger! Is it to be observed every year?' The Prophet was furious and said: 'By Allah, if I said yes, it would be compulsory, and if it becomes compulsory, you will not be able to do it (pilgrimage), and you will then disbelieve in it. So, do not ask me about things which I have left out, and comply with what I*

---

[299]     *Muhammad, Messenger of Allah: Ash-Shifa of Qadi 'Iyad*, p. 216.

[300]     *Tafsir Ibn Kathir*, Vol. 3, p. 282.

*ordered you to do and abstain from what I have
forbidden.'"* [301]

And Muhammad even said that asking about something could have
negative consequences by resulting in its subsequent prohibition:

> *Narrated Sa'd bin Abi Waqqas: The Prophet said, "The
> worst in crime among the Muslims is the one who asked
> about something which had not been prohibited, but was
> prohibited because of his asking."* [302]

---

[301]    *Tafsir Ibn Kathir*, Part 7, p. 66.

[302]    *Sahih Al-Bukhari*, Vol. 9, Book 96, No. 7289, p. 240.  This narration by
Sa'd was also reported in *Sahih Muslim*, Vol. 7, No. 2358, p. 52.

# Appendix 2: Abu Hurairah

Abu Hurairah converted to Islam just prior to the conquest of Khaybar in May 628, became a close companion of Muhammad, and remained so until Muhammad's death on June 7, 632. Abu Hurairah was renowned for the number of *hadiths* he reported.[303]

In the following *hadiths* we find Muhammad proclaiming that

1. The only way non-Muslims could save themselves was by converting to Islam;

2. Even the rocks would call out for Muslims to kill Jews; and

3. Obeying him was not only the same as obeying Allah, but was also the way to get into Paradise.

These statements of Muhammad would have been made during the time period of May 628 to June 632, well after 2:256 (No Compulsion) was "revealed" in August 625:

1. *Narrated Abu Hurairah: Allah's Messenger said, "I have been ordered (by Allah) to fight against the people till they say La ilaha illallah (none has the right to be worshipped but Allah), and whoever said La ilaha illallah, he saved his life and property from*

---

[303]     *Men and Women Around the Messenger*, pp. 323-324.

*me except for Islamic law, and his accounts will be
with Allah (either to punish him or to forgive him).* "[304]

2. *Narrated Abu Hurairah: While we were in the
mosque, the Prophet came out and said, "Let us go to
the Jews." We went out till we reached Bait-ul-
Midras. He said to them, "If you embrace Islam, you
will be safe. You should know that the earth belongs
to Allah and His Messenger, and I want to expel you
from this land. So, if anyone amongst you owns some
property, he is permitted to sell it, otherwise you
should know that the earth belongs to Allah and His
Messenger.*[305]

3. *Narrated Abu Hurairah: Allah's Messenger said,
"The Hour will not be established until you fight
against the Jews, and the stone behind which a Jew
will be hiding will say, 'O Muslim! There is a Jew
hiding behind me, so kill him.'"*[306]

4. *It was narrated that Abu Hurairah said: "The
Messenger of Allah said, 'Whatever I have
commanded you, do it, and whatever I have forbidden
you, refrain from it.'"*[307]

---

[304]    *Sahih Al-Bukhari*, Vol. 4, Book 56, No. 2946, p. 126. This statement by
Abu Hurairah was similarly reported in *Musnad Imam Ahmad Bin Hanbal*, Vol. 1,
No. 67, pp. 58-59.

[305]    *Sahih Al-Bukhari*, Vol. 4, Book 58, No. 3167, p. 248. A longer version
of this *hadith* was reported in *Sahih Al-Bukhari*, Vol. 9, Book 89, No. 6944, pp.
60-61; and Vol. 9, Book 96, No. 7348, pp. 268-269. This *hadith* was also reported
in *Sahih Muslim*, Vol. 5, No. 1765, p. 186.

[306]    *Sahih Al-Bukhari*, Vol. 4, Book 56, No. 2926, p. 113.

[307]    *Sunan Ibn Majah*, Vol. 1, No. 1, p. 73.

5. *Narrated Abu Hurairah: Allah's Messenger said, "Whoever obeys me, he obeys Allah, and whoever disobeys me, he disobeys Allah; and whoever obeys my ruler (the ruler I appoint) he obeys me, and whoever disobeys my (appointed) ruler, he disobeys me.*[308]

6. *Narrated Abu Hurairah: Allah's Messenger said, "All my followers will enter Paradise except those who refuse." They (the people) asked, "O Allah's Messenger! Who will refuse?" He said, "Whoever obeys me will enter Paradise, and whoever disobeys me is the one who refuses (to enter it)."*[309]

---

[308]    *Sahih Al-Bukhari*, Vol. 9, Book 93, No. 7137, p. 160.

[309]    Ibid., Book 96, No. 7280, p. 235.

# Bibliography
## (Arranged by title)

Muhammad ibn 'Abdul Wahhab at-Tamimi, *Abridged Biography of Prophet Muhammad*, ed. 'Abdur-Rahman bin Nasir Al-Barrak, 'Abdul 'Azeez bin 'Abdullah Ar-Rajihi, and Muhammad Al-'Ali Al-Barrak (Riyadh, Kingdom of Saudi Arabia: Darussalam, 2003)

Malik ibn Anas ibn Malik ibn Abi 'Amir al-Asbahi, *Al-Muwatta of Imam Malik ibn Anas: The First Formulation of Islamic Law*, trans. Aisha Abdurrahman Bewley (Inverness, Scotland: Madinah Press, 2004)

Abu'l-Hasan 'Ali ibn Ahmad ibn Muhammad ibn 'Ali al-Wahidi, *Al-Wahidi's Asbab al-Nuzul*, trans. Mokrane Guezzou (Louisville, KY: Fons Vitae, 2008)

Abu Ammaar Yasir Qadhi, *An Introduction to the Sciences of the Qur'aan* (Birmingham, UK: Al-Hidaayah Publishing, 1999)

Mahmoud Ismail Saleh, *Dictionary of Islamic Words & Expressions*, 3rd ed. (Riyadh, Kingdom of Saudi Arabia: Darussalam, 2011)

'Imaduddeen Isma'eel ibn Katheer al-Qurashi, *In Defence of the True Faith: Battles, Expeditions, Peace Treaties and their Consequences in the life of Prophet Muhammad*, trans. Research Department of Darussalam (Riyadh, Kingdom of Saudi Arabia: Darussalam, 2010)

147

*Interpretation of the Meanings of The Noble Qur'an*, trans. Muhammad Muhsin Khan and Muhammad Taqi-ud-Din Al-Hilali (Riyadh, Kingdom of Saudi Arabia: Darussalam, 2007)

Ahmad ibn Abdul-Halim ibn Taymiyyah, *Introduction to the Principles of Tafsir*, Explanation by Shaykh Muhammad ibn Salih al-Uthaymin (Birmingham, UK: Al-Hidaayah Publishing, 2009)

Abu 'Eisa Mohammad ibn 'Eisa at-Tirmidhi, *Jami' At-Tirmidhi*, trans. Abu Khaliyl, 6 Volumes (Riyadh, Kingdom of Saudi Arabia: Darussalam, 2007)

Abu 'Abd Allah Muhammad ibn Sa'd ibn Mani' al-Zuhri al-Basri, *Kitab al-Tabaqat al-Kabir*, Vols. 1 and 2, trans. S. Moinul Haq (New Delhi, India: Kitab Bhavan, 2009)

Sa'd Yusuf Abu 'Aziz, *Men and Women Around the Messenger*, trans. Suleman Fulani (Riyadh, Kingdom of Saudi Arabia: Darussalam, 2009)

Qadi 'Iyad ibn Musa al-Yahsubi, *Muhammad, Messenger of Allah: Ash-Shifa of Qadi 'Iyad*, trans. Aisha Abdarrahman Bewley (Norwich, UK: Diwan Press, 2011)

Ahmad bin Muhammad bin Hanbal ash-Shaibani, *Musnad Imam Ahmad Bin Hanbal*, trans. Nasiruddin Al-Khattab, ed. Huda Al-Khattab, 3 Volumes (Riyadh, Kingdom of Saudi Arabia: Darussalam, 2012)

*Pakistan Blasphemy Laws, Ending the Abuse of the Blasphemy Laws*, http://www.pakistanblasphemylaw.com/?page_id=15

Muhammad bin Ismail bin Al-Mughirah al-Bukhari, *Sahih Al-Bukhari*, trans. Muhammad Muhsin Khan, 9 Volumes (Riyadh, Kingdom of Saudi Arabia: Darussalam, 1997)

Abu'l Hussain 'Asakir-ud-Din Muslim bin Hajjaj al-Qushayri al-Naisaburi, *Sahih Muslim*, trans. 'Abdul Hamid Siddiqi, 8 Volumes (New Delhi, India: Adam Publishers and Distributors, 2008)

Abu Dawud Sulaiman bin al-Ash'ath bin Ishaq, *Sunan Abu Dawud*, trans. Yaser Qadhi, 5 Volumes (Riyadh, Kingdom of Saudi Arabia: Darussalam, 2008)

Abu 'Abdur-Rahman Ahmad bin Shu'aib bin 'Ali bin Sinan bin Bahr An-Nasa'i, *Sunan An-Nasa'i*, trans. Nasiruddin al-Khattab, 6 Volumes (Riyadh, Kingdom of Saudi Arabia: Darussalam, 2007)

Muhammad bin Yazeed ibn Majah al-Qazwini, *Sunan Ibn Majah*, trans. Nasiruddin al-Khattab, 5 Volumes (Riyadh, Kingdom of Saudi Arabia: Darussalam, 2007)

Salahuddin Yusuf, *Tafsir Ahsanul-Bayan*, trans. Mohammad Kamal Myshkat, 5 Volumes (Riyadh, Kingdom of Saudi Arabia: Darussalam, 2010)

Jalalu'd-Din al-Mahalli and Jalalu'd-Din as-Suyuti, *Tafsir Al-Jalalayn*, trans. Aisha Bewley (London: Dar Al Taqwa Ltd., 2007)

Abu 'Abdullah Muhammad ibn Ahmad al-Ansari al-Qurtubi, *Tafsir Al-Qurtubi: Classical Commentary of the Holy Qur'an*, Vol. 1, trans. Aisha Bewley (London: Dar Al Taqwa Ltd., 2003)

149

'Abd ar-Rahman b. Nasir as-Sa'di, *Tafsir As-Sa'di*, trans. S. Abd al-Hamid, Vol. 1 (Floral Park, New York: The Islamic Literary Foundation: 2012)

'Abd ar-Rahman b. Nasir as-Sa'di, *Tafsir As-Sa'di*, trans. S. Abd al-Hamid, Vol. 2 (Floral Park, New York: The Islamic Literary Foundation: 2014)

*Tafsir Ibn 'Abbas*, trans. Mokrane Guezzou (Louisville, KY: Fons Vitae, 2008)

Abu al-Fida' 'Imad Ad-Din Isma'il bin 'Umar bin Kathir al-Qurashi Al-Busrawi, *Tafsir Ibn Kathir* (Abridged), 11 Parts, abr. Sheikh Muhammad Nasib Ar-Rafa'i, trans. Chafik Abdelghani ibn Rahal (London: Al-Firdous Ltd., 1998)

Abu al-Fida' 'Imad Ad-Din Isma'il bin 'Umar bin Kathir al-Qurashi Al-Busrawi, *Tafsir Ibn Kathir* (Abridged), 10 Volumes, abr. Shaykh Safiur-Rahman al-Mubarakpuri, trans. Jalal Abualrub, et al. (Riyadh, Kingdom of Saudi Arabia: Darussalam, 2000)

Ma'mar ibn Rashid, *The Expeditions (Kitab al-Maghazi)*, trans. Sean W. Anthony (New York: New York University Press/Library of Arabic Literature, 2014)

Abu Ja'far Muhammad b. Jarir al-Tabari, *The History of al-Tabari: Muhammad at Mecca*, Vol. VI, trans. and annotated W. Montgomery Watt and M. V. McDonald (Albany, New York: State University of New York Press, 1988)

Abu Ja'far Muhammad b. Jarir al-Tabari, *The History of al-Tabari: The Foundation of the Community*, Vol. VII, trans. and annotated W. Montgomery Watt and M. V. McDonald (Albany, New York: State University of New York Press, 1987)

Abu Ja'far Muhammad b. Jarir al-Tabari, *The History of al-Tabari: The Last Years of the Prophet*, Vol. IX, trans. and annotated Ismail K. Poonawala (Albany, New York: State University of New York Press, 1990)

Abu Ja'far Muhammad b. Jarir al-Tabari, *The History of al-Tabari: The Victory of Islam*, Vol. VIII, trans. and annotated Michael Fishbein (Albany, New York: State University of New York Press, 1997)

*The Honourable Wives of the Prophet*, ed. Abdul Ahad (Riyadh, Kingdom of Saudi Arabia: Darussalam, 2004)

Muhammad b. 'Umar al-Waqidi, *The Life of Muhammad: Al-Waqidi's Kitab al-Maghazi*, trans. Rizwi Faizer, Amal Ismail, and AbdulKader Tayob, ed. Rizwi Faizer (London and New York: Routledge, 2013)

Muhammad ibn Ishaq, *The Life of Muhammad (Sirat Rasul Allah)*, trans. Alfred Guillaume (Karachi, Pakistan: Oxford University Press, 2007)

*The Meaning of the Glorious Koran*, trans. Marmaduke Pickthall (1930; rpt. New York: Alfred A. Knopf, 1992)

*The Muslim 500 – The World's 500 Most Influential Muslims 2016*, The Royal Islamic Strategic Studies Centre (Amman, Jordan)

Ahmad ibn Yahya ibn Jabir al-Baladhuri, *The Origins of the Islamic State, Being a Translation from the Arabic, Accompanied with Annotations, Geographic and Historic Notes of the Kitab Fituh Al-Buldan of Al-Imam Abu-L Abbas Ahmad Ibn-Jabir Al-Baladhuri*, trans. Philip Khuri Hitti (1916; rpt. Lexington, Kentucky: Ulan Press, 2014)

Jalal-al-Din 'Abd al-Rahman al-Suyuti, *The Perfect Guide to the Sciences of the Qur'an*, trans. Hamid Algar, et al. (Reading, UK: Garnet Publishing, 2011)

Safiur-Rahman al-Mubarakpuri, *The Sealed Nectar* (Riyadh, Kingdom of Saudi Arabia: Darussalam, 2008)

Ahmad Von Denffer, *'Ulum al-Qur'an: An Introduction to the Sciences of the Qur'an* (Leicestershire, UK: The Islamic Foundation, 1994)

Safiur Rahman Mubarakpuri, *When the Moon Split* (Riyadh, Kingdom of Saudi Arabia: Darussalam, 2009)

'Imaduddeen Isma'eel ibn Katheer al-Qurashi, *Winning the Hearts and Souls: Expeditions and Delegations in the Lifetime of Prophet Muhammad*, trans. Research Department of Darussalam (Riyadh, Kingdom of Saudi Arabia: Darussalam, 2010)

Made in the USA
Columbia, SC
29 October 2017